D0984494

COLERIDGE AND S.T.C.

COLERIDGE AND S.T.C.

BY

STEPHEN POTTER

New York
RUSSELL & RUSSELL
1965

FIRST PUBLISHED IN 1935
REISSUED, 1965, BY RUSSELL & RUSSELL, INC.
BY ARRANGEMENT WITH STEPHEN POTTER
L.C. CATALOG CARD NO: 65—18827
PRINTED IN THE UNITED STATES OF AMERICA

CONTENTS

COLERIDGE AND S.T.C.

COLERIDGE AND S.T.C.

I KNOW that the discovery which I describe in this
book is not new; that the fact that there are two Coleridges is the first discovery of almost every reader. I
know also that it is true that in another sense Coleridge is multiple. He is one of those few writers whose
scale is as large and as many-dimensioned as a
phenomenon of nature, so that while the reader
grows, as his world unfolds, his Coleridge alters with
it. For myself, Coleridge was first of all not even
Coleridge. In the dark ages of childhood, when works
of art are anonymous, he was *The Ancient Mariner*. Nor
was *The Ancient Mariner* so much a poem as a book
with pictures, illustrated in the kindly grotesque
manner of 1910—Rackham- rather than Coleridge-
supernatural. Time passes. Coleridge becomes associated—in late teens, perhaps—with a first response
to poetry. He is *Poet* as early conceived, untouch-
able and mysterious. Personal interest is awakened,
and a third Coleridge begins to appear, a Coleridge
of disconnected phrases picked up from book-loving
aunt, university education in the arts, literary articles
in newspapers. Drifting facts attach themselves to
the mind : *Launched into his subject like an eagle dallying*

with the wind . . . 1798 . . . Dorothy Wordsworth and her
Journal . . . Coleridge taking poetical images from her
(interesting fact) . . . poetic diction, C. right, Wordsworth
wrong . . . secret ministry of frost . . . Kubla Khan—due to
drugs . . . metaphysics—pity to give up poetry for . . .
damaged archangel . . . never used talents—due to drugs . . .
but Table Talk . . . but Carlyle . . . Coleridge sat on the
brow of Highgate Hill . . . Gillman . . . drugs. Such
phrases have their power. They and their like settle
into a preconception which casual reading will not
get beyond. Further metamorphoses are reserved for
the professional student perhaps, the unprofessional
explorer more likely, the steadfast reader, the enthusiastic editor. For the editor, for instance, there is an
object-Coleridge, a physical residue, the taste, strongly
individual and not especially palatable, of the literary
remains. Prose and blank verse pages heavy with
unbroken print, mercilessly devoid of 'fat,' relieved
only by a monotonous variation of capital letter and
italic. Handwriting without charm, of a clerkly slope
and an unclerkly illegibility—illegibility due not to
bad writing but to a taste for writing under difficulties,
for wedging a parenthesis into a page already packed,
or for writing the most voluble criticisms in the nar-
rowest margins of the book which calls them forth.

'Characteristic,' it will be said. For if the possible
shapes which he may assume are as numerous as
there are types to behold them, there is one side of
Coleridge on which all assiduous readers are agreed—
his character. The lengthier the studies, the more
various the aspects which come under view, the more

unambiguously does a character stand out—not an especially admirable character, not even a very lovable one, but unique, and described with unexampled lack of reticence.

I have been familiar with this character for some time—have specially studied it, seeing in its weakness, as so many others have done, a useful re-statement of my own. But the most valuable, the most surprising discovery of my reading life has been of a further Coleridge still, beyond the character, a side with which the character has only a chance, or fatal connection.

Because this Coleridge cannot be summarised, because he varies for each discoverer, I have written this book. If I had to put my own realisation in a phrase it would be that—his words have meaning. That these long, hortatory, exculpatory sentences have meaning.

Once known, seeming always to have been known: nevertheless it is the fact one is likely to learn last. The words and phrases he uses seem at first reading imageless, like the more colourless serious writing of his time, but without its Johnsonian trenchancy. It is only in their context that they have this meaning, and the context of the page, the context of the book even, is not sufficient. In his writings the originality lies not in the word, but in the user of the word. Coleridge (to the neophyte it is a damping fact) must be read in some sort of entirety before he can be read fruitfully, if only because he was continuously changing, so that there is a context of process besides a context of immediate meaning. He has a drift, in fact, and it is only when read with reference to their drift that his words 'excite a feeling analogous to the supernatural by awakening the mind's attention from the lethargy of custom.' Without the drift, we are aware of a Character, and nothing more.

My object is to show how this developing *Coleridge*, and this intrusive Character, exist together. My theme is duality—a theme interesting and important not because of its uniqueness, but because of its universality, since all men know that in some sense they are possessed of twofold selves. The Jekyll and Hyde story seems to us to have the ancient quality of a myth, worlds removed from its modern author, because it is a perpetual analogy of our own condition. The story of humanity reverting to beasthood is a precise parable of the evolutionary sequel to that situation—superhumanity checked by the constant regression, the constant relapse, to the all-too-human.

But if the theme is not new, neither is there any novelty in my choice of an example. Indeed it is famous that the outward appearance of Coleridge fits the case. His own description of it—'indolence capable of energies'—agrees with the world's, as does his own epitomisation of his features—'the brow of an angel, and the mouth of a beast'—except that for 'beast' the world substituted more derogatory, less Hyde-like words. 'Nothing can convey stronger indications of power than his eye, eyebrow, and forehead. Nothing can be more *imbecile* than all the rest of his face.'

But the question arises—are these old physiological signposts trustworthy? May not the weak mouth, with weakly pendulous lips (Coleridge suffered from bad teeth and an inability to breathe through his nose), be as undependable for purposes of diagnosis as the honest eye? This kind of character-reading is likely to demonstrate such a man weak-willed (judging 'will-power,' perhaps, by the standard of the Wellington profile) without more than the most rudimentary notion of what the word 'will' can signify. And it is just that kind of character-fixer who is likely to think of traits as always arranged in neatly opposed groups—genius opposed to the methodical, etc.

'Great injury has resulted from the supposed incompatibility of one talent with another.'

However it may be, the duality of Coleridge has come under rigid interpretation on the lines of Weak Genius; and the problem is further over-simplified by the tendency of the antagonistic criticism of his contemporaries, the key of which is set by Hazlitt, with his essays in the 'Then' and 'Now' vein. The implication in Hazlitt, of course, is that the Coleridge of his youthful reminiscence, in whom poetry and philosophy were met together, is entirely admirable, whereas the Coleridge of his middle age, producing bogus sermons in the intervals of drug debauchery, is all bad. It would be interesting to trace how often it happens that the world's stock judgments follow the first firm critical statement by an articulate contemporary.

The kind of question begging in such statements of the case is so beyond argument, the implications so false, that this picture of Coleridge's duality must be allowed to pass undisproven. It is not in the Hazlitt

15

or Southey way of looking at things that the two-sidedness of Coleridge is a universal two-sidedness. 'Weak will and decay . . .' With all their talents, in the world neither of Southey nor Hazlitt did the kind of will Coleridge was capable of exercising exist, nor the kind of evolution without which neither decay nor development is possible.

The real distinction, it seems to me, lies in the opposition between 'character' and 'personality.' In other words, between ego and Self. In Blake's words, between Self and Identity. In other words, between the continuously evolving, experiencing, truly living person, and the fixed character back into which each successive metamorphosis tends to relapse. Coleridge was fully possessed of this true self, with all its powers of experience, change, uniqueness, differentiation from the common stock: he was also possessed *by* a particularly formidable, strongly marked character. One of its traits happened to be weakness, but if that trait could have been, as it sometimes is, reversible, the handicap would have been no less. It was only when he was able to transcend the character, to shake off this Old Man of the Sea, that he was himself, and it is the hamperings of this character, and the successful if incomplete emancipation of his true self, which I want to describe.

*

There are certain factors which make Coleridge a good subject for this kind of study. First of all, he was an autobiographical writer, in almost every sense in which that ambiguous description can be used. For instance, the *Biographia Literaria* is not the only work of his which gives an account of his own opinions—nor is his literary life more the theme than his *biographia religiosa, metaphysica,* etc. He was interested in the facts of his own life (*cf.* the early auto-biographical letters to Poole). He believed in the importance of biography in general:

> I could inform the dullest author how he might write an interesting book. Let him relate the events of his own life with honesty, not disguising the feelings that accompanied them. I never yet read even a Methodist's Experience in the *Gospel Magazine* without receiving instruction and amusement. (525)

He himself had all the necessary acquirements of the natural autobiographer. He was a notebook man. He had the instinct to record, and the instinct not to destroy records. He had an instinctive dread of burning paper, and is ashamed to confess to a 'pulling back of the heart' whenever he wished to 'light a candle or kindle a fire with a Hospital or Harbour Report.'[1] But much stronger than his instinct to record was his impulse to *express*—stronger than his human feelings of reticence, stronger than his desire to be respected, liked, judged kindly, was his desire to *tell*, to *speak*. In letters, in parentheses, in relevant footnotes to irrelevant texts, he holds up his heart in full view, so loaded with feeling, and with a consciousness of Self so strong, that self-consciousness melts away. Once or twice he apologises. 'We are soothed by communications,' he

[1] *A.P.*, 121.

pleads. Partly, he is unloading miseries. Partly, he is trying to know them. 'In relating what ails us, we ourselves first know exactly what the real grief is, and see it for itself in its own form and limits.'[1]

Partly, his interest and pleasure in each new thing, every change in his life, works such a transformation in him, that he has to confide this, too.

Put it a little differently, allow the facts to group themselves naturally, and see that Coleridge is a rare and perfect example of twofold autobiographer. Charles Lamb or Montaigne can present traits: their writings are a long character-study. This is one kind of autobiography which Coleridge achieves; and because there is less reserve—less art, if you like—about him, the character is fuller, less related to known world types, more individual, with less of a personal ideal about it, than that which these great essayists have revealed.

But Coleridge's writings contain another kind of biography also. Never quite severed from life, he developed and changed, passing through the stages of more than one metamorphosis. Goethe exemplifies the pure type of this kind of continuity: his works record pure development, pure differences, pure creation.

But, just as in Montaigne the life is described from one unchanging point of human nature, so on the other side does Goethe seem only to write from the depths of himself. The fixed character, the human side, seems transcended. The opposition in Goethe is

[1] *A.P.*, 32.

between the become and the becoming, the experienced and the yet to be experienced.

In Coleridge, character and development exist side by side. The opposition is between the human and the superhuman. Humphry Davy was wrong to say that it was Coleridge's *habit* to write 'from the depth of his being.'[1] But the depths were there, and suddenly, in the midst of the more automatic character record, will come a voice from this other Coleridge world, making character irrelevant. A Johnson or a Montaigne will be dangerously happy in the possession of his so effective character—each, moreover, is so completely armed with word ramparts that nothing but the character emerges. Scarcely a hint is allowed to escape of the potentially differing, inconsistent Person beneath. But with Coleridge, in whom thought and word were one, Personality appears with the personal: with Coleridge, who was uncontrollably expressive, Godlike and human are shown together.

In this book I try to describe, and to distinguish, these two sides of Coleridge, disentangling them from a sometimes mutually obliterating embrace. Character interests and fascinates me; but Personality, the mystery of absolute difference in men, concerns me. I try to learn from Goethe that mankind does not exist, only men. Character belongs to mankind. I am concerned with 'Coleridge,' and I describe his character as well only because it was not until I had described it to myself and understood its separate existence that

[1] J.D., 74.

'Coleridge,' belonging not to mankind but to men, became clear to me.

To avoid the barbarous awkwardness, in the following pages, of using words like 'real self,' 'inner self,' on the one hand, and 'outward self,' 'fixed character,' on the other, I have invented names: 'Coleridge' for the developing Personality, and 'S.T.C.' for the fixed character.

The choice is not quite arbitrary. Coleridge had strong views about names. 'Hartley,' 'Berkeley,' 'Derwent,' 'Sara'—all had very special significance. Of his own names, he detested 'Samuel.'[1] Of his nicknames, he doesn't seem to have taken to the early abbreviation 'Col.'; but, on the other hand, 'S.T.C.' he loved. 'S.T.C.' was his favourite, the name he wished to be known by. It is the title of his latest verses (an 'epitaph on a poet little known, yet better known by the initials of his name than by the name itself'). The wish seems father to the thought. Coleridge cannot be placed among that attractive class whom it is natural to call by their initials. The famous secret is given away when Coleridge spells the name in Greek capitals, thus: *ΕΣΤΗΣΗ*—what he called 'Punnic' Greek for 'he stands firm.'

---

[1] *Cf. L.* 470: From my earliest years I have had a feeling of dislike and disgust connected with my own Christian name—such a vile short plumpness, such a dull abortive smartness in the first syllable, and this so harshly contrasted by the obscurity and indefiniteness of the syllabic vowel, and the feebleness of the uncovered liquid with which it ends, the wobble it makes, and struggling between a dis- and a tri-syllable, and the whole name sounding as if you were abeeceeing S.M.U.L. Altogether, it is, perhaps, the worst combination of which vowels and consonants are susceptible.

COLERIDGE AND S.T.C.

Since the only firm thing about Coleridge is the regrettable permanence of the fixed character, I have chosen 'S.T.C.' for this aspect. It fits in rather well, also, with C.'s picture of himself; a kind of ideal which was peculiarly unlike, and inferior to, himself. 'Coleridge' I am keeping for the other. It is a beautiful name, mysterious and dignified—even if (since Coleridge was the master of euphony) we have to bow to his wish that it should be pronounced with a strong hint of three syllables, and the 'o' short.

Thorough-going psychologists won't, I hope, think ill of these terms and categories. I believe that a psychopathic treatment of Coleridge should prove an illuminating description, or parable, of the truth. I have avoided such angles of approach here. I should hesitate to use them, even if I had the necessary knowledge, because of the contemporary tendency to regard such descriptions as explanations.

Reading them through I am appalled, for my own sake, at the goodness in these pages. It lies in the quotations; and as often happens in this kind of criticism by significant arrangements of texts, the potency of these seems to sun the colour out of the elucidatory comments which surround them, made more pallid already by the spacing of the print. Nevertheless, it is no good reading Coleridge in quotations. Their meaning will be lost unless the general drift is perceived. This it is which the Coleridge critic may try to indicate. This drift, the direction of the stream, and the impediments and *diverticula* in its course, I try to describe.

2

COLERIDGE

GREAT English writers are numerous: the native talent runs that way. Which to choose? And (the English way of writing so faithful to its acknowledged merits as it is)—how to differentiate? There is almost certain to be image-evoking description, some hitherto unnoted object neatly ringed by some surprise adjective; rich descriptions of old England, or astringent of modern; observant character studies, a clerk or an innkeeper captured for ever; daring minuteness of touches, humour; and nature work—the grandeur of rocks, the desirability of turf, the peacefulness of lawns are more likely to be described than not. Sometimes it scarcely seems to matter who is chosen—except for the reader with an appetite for growth, for a clarification of past experience, and for an education in knowledge, feeling, and passion of the kind which will make further experience possible. The difficulty then is to find among these great excellencies a man—a great man.

I seem to be begging an important question. 'There is more than one kind of greatness'—Goethe is reproving Eckermann for questioning his praise of Byron. He implies that there are great privy councillors, besides great artists; great romantic figures besides great writers. But he would not have denied that there are also great men, who, like Byron, may be, who often are, in complete possession of one of man's attributes. Nevertheless, the distinguishing mark of a great man a Byron does not possess—the ability to live continuously, which involves the ability to grow, and all the sowing and reaping processes of experience: the phenomenon of growth continued through life, with which Byronic primrose paths and reformations have no connection.

The principal evidence for 'Coleridge' is the fact that Coleridge evolved. Whether or no he was a great writer is a large and cloudy problem. What is certain is that he possessed a Life, out of the context of dates, or sequence of external events—a life of the kind potential in all, and for that reason worth study and elucidation above all other qualities in genius.

All know that Coleridge changed. But the accepted account of this change is part of the picturesque Coleridge tradition, and implies nothing of evolution. Pantisocracy . . . Poetry . . . Metaphysics is its outline. Wild-oats . . . 'flowering' high-spot of genius . . . regrettable decline into abstractions. Changes in opinion can also be quoted, changes brought about by health, or drug-effects, or the physical atrophies of age.

Another kind of picture, much more representative of Coleridge's real development, is given by students of his philosophy in their accounts of the genealogy of his opinions and successive beliefs. Such accounts, presented illuminatingly by Shawcross and Muirhead,

23

I am making much use of. Yet these also can be misleading unless they are explained and understood as a reflection of growth, unless the point is belaboured again that when Coleridge incorporates a new philosophy, or a view associated with a recently studied book—that when he allows Kant, or Wordsworth, to 'take hold of him with giant hands,' he is not subject to influence, in the generally accepted sense of the term: 'exfluence' would be better. He adopts the ideas not because he finds them striking, but because his reading of the book, or his meeting with the new friend, corresponds with some accession of consciousness on his part. Coleridge was influenced because he was capable of influence. He who all through his life 'read everything' was capable of allowing each direction of his growth to be made more explicit and given point by the records of co-experiencers.

At this point a preliminary dip into the Coleridge ocean will help to acclimatise:

O! it requires deeper feeling, and a stronger imagination, than belongs to most of those, to whom reasoning and fluent expression have been as a trade learnt in boyhood, to conceive with what *might*, with what inward *strivings* and *commotion*, the perception of a new and vital TRUTH takes possession of an uneducated man of genius. (*B.L.*, i. 97)

Here Coleridge, in spite of 'uneducated,' is generalising from the pristine quality of his own sensations. No wonder his friends failed to pin him down to a consistent doctrine. No wonder Mrs. Coleridge was bewildered, writing to Poole that she did not know how properly to reply ('pray furnish me') when she was asked, as she was often asked, if Coleridge had changed his political sentiments.

For Coleridge did not change his opinions. He did not proceed by a series of emancipations, a kind of career in which the fetters always seem more in evidence than the enfranchisement. He did not look back patronisingly on former stages through which he had passed. He more than once speaks of his disgust at a recantation:

> Why do we so very, very often see men pass from one extreme to the other? Alas! they sought not the truth, but praise, self-importance, and above all [the sense of] something doing! Disappointed, they hate and persecute their former opinion, which no man will do who by meditation had adopted it, and in the course of unfeigned meditation gradually enlarged the circle and so got out of it. (168)

With the image of 'enlarging the circle' in mind, and with proud humility proper to a first attempt, I will suggest an evolution of Coleridge.

*

Coleridge was born in 1772, but according to the natural process 'Coleridge' did not make his appearance till after adolescence. Yet this adolescence of Coleridge, though normal and typical, was a strange prefiguration of the life to follow. There was, for instance, a proto-intellectualist stage linked with schoolboy talents as precocious as talents usually are. He was atheist, Voltairean, age-of-Reason, 'startled at fifteen' by the arguments of Dr. Darwin against God[1] —intellectualism which included the reading of the neoplatonists at school, and which led him at Cambridge to allow his rooms to be the meeting ground of the Supporters of Frend, the centre of Cambridge emancipation, liberal Foxite views in politics, and emancipated Unitarianism in religion. Then this dress-rehearsal of a first step was followed by a little embryonic act of growth. Poetry and feeling began to take the place of metaphysical controversy, from which Coleridge says he was 'auspiciously withdrawn'

> by the genial influence of a style of poetry, so tender and yet so manly, so natural and real, and yet so dignified and harmonious, as the sonnets, etc., of Mr. Bowles! (214)

Poetry, it will be seen, of a qualified kind: part of conventional youth's idea of what poetry ought to be— solemn, serene, manly, 'beautiful,' general. And then, finally, comes a little wild-oat sowing. Obscure, rather scrambled weeks when he seems to have struggled, awkwardly, to conform to Regency manners. Debts. A luxury of shame for Coleridge, a melancholy for love unreturned, and a sweeping departure from the world. He enlists. He will lose himself in a foreign land (there were family precedents for this), laid low, perhaps, by an alien hand. All leading inevitably to

---

[1] *B.L.*, i. xii.

repentance, and prostration before brother George—
prostration and confession:

> I fled to debauchery; fled pure silent and solitary
> Anguish to all the uproar of senseless mirth . . .
> for the whole six weeks . . . I was almost constantly
> intoxicated! My Brother! you shudder as you read.
> . . . Where Vice has not annihilated sensibility,
> there is little need of a Hell!   (540)

This is the false dawn of Coleridge's life. Now might
Coleridge well have settled down, facing the practical
tasks of life, feeling that he had done his duty by its
ardours. Or he might have become a political or
literary figure, with Frend, or Bowles, as hero:

> in poetry as well as metaphysics, that which we
> first meet with in the dawn of our mind becomes
> ever after *fetish*, to the many at least.   (180)

With two or three such *fetishes*, Coleridge could have
retired for life, not only with the sense that he was an
old hand in point of experience, but with a feeling
of comfortable emancipation as well.

*

But the event was different. If only more detail
were available there would be nothing in biography
more worth describing than the way in which Coleridge dismissed these preliminaries, to turn to life as
if for the first time. I think this first chapter in the
life of 'Coleridge' should start with a quotation from
a letter, written in the year 1794:

It is wrong, Southey! for a little girl with a half-famished sickly baby in her arms to put her head in at the window of an inn—'Pray give me a bit of bread and meat!' from a party dining on lamb, green peas, and salad. Why? Because it is impertinent and obtrusive! 'I am a gentleman! and wherefore the clamorous voice of woe intrude upon mine ear?' My companion is a man of cultivated, though not vigorous understanding; his feelings are all on the side of humanity; yet such are the unfeeling remarks, which the lingering remains of aristocracy occasionally prompt. When the pure system of pantisocracy shall have aspheterized—from ἀ, non, and σφέτερος proprius. . . .   (543)

The name 'Pantisocracy,' Coleridge's language in this letter and other letters; the likelihood that his enthusiasm for the Susquehannah as a site for his community was influenced by a recommendation from a son-in-law of Priestley; the Godwinian nature of some of the details of his plan—all seem to make this new enthusiasm one piece with the leftish young undergraduate writing poems on the Bastille a year or so before. But though the cast of his thought is the same, Coleridge, the ore in the cast, was entirely different. It all seemed, and therefore was, something which had never happened before. 'I am neither Jacobin nor Democrat, but a Pantisocrat,'[1] was his pertinent answer to the reproofs of the Master of Jesus. It was something absolutely different, he wanted to make

[1] J.D.C., 41.
28

clear, from the advanced political *notions* which he had been learning from Godwin and Frend.

It was what Coleridge was later to call a Principle. The first Idea in his life. There is nothing original in the schemes which Coleridge drew up. The political philosophy of it would seem to fit in with Godwinian beliefs that evil is the direct cause of bad government, or bad environment, only: the ethic of it—that acting in accordance with the good of the whole is the only way to act with true self-interest—seems part of the popular and hollow ethic of the day; Locke, Tucker, and the 'pursuit of happiness'; Utilitarianism. Nevertheless, Pantisocracy is unique. Coleridge apprehends its principle as an Idea to be incorporated in life and expressed in action. To assert to the abstract proposition of it is not enough. Coleridge is now capable of something more than assertion. 'It is not enough,' he says, 'that we have once swallowed it. The heart should have fed upon the truth, as insects on a leaf, till it be tinged with the colour, and show its food in every the minutest fibre.'[1] The voice of 'Coleridge,' thus articulate already in the autumn of 1794, shows that his purpose was individuality, not happiness, a commonwealth not for the people, but for persons. It was a principle that he was earning the right to formulate, now that individuality was beginning to show in himself.

Life seemed to be mounting irresistibly in him at this time. No wonder, that looking back on it, he calls Pantisocracy 'the fairest of all fair dreams'; that every-

[1] 549.

thing he does and writes at this time, even the strangely inexpressive verses, cannot be criticised by him in later life for their intrinsic value: for him they are saturated with a meaning strongly felt, but not yet articulate. It was not a dream. This is the time which in retrospect reminded him of a rarely felt Hope, the sense of effective action, which now 'grew round and upheld him like the twining vine.' To realise this youth of Coleridge is to realise how few are ever young, or how much more typical cynicism, diffidence, pedantry can be of the time of life when the impulse to rush for safety is almost as strong as the desire to forget safety in new and perilous growth. But Coleridge really was young in his youth—may be immortal for this if for no other reason—really attained youthful Idealism, the pursuit of a purpose made valuable by the unquestioning and lively certainty of the pursuer.

O! the one Life within us and abroad,
Which meets all motion and becomes its soul,
A light in sound, a sound-like power in light,
Rhythm in all thought, and joyance every where—
Methinks, it should have been impossible
Not to love all things in a world so filled. (*P.*, 101)

This power is reflected in its effect on his friends. Either they were blown, protesting, aside, or sucked along in the draught he was creating. Southey, for instance, was temporarily swept from his conventionally promising career, balanced precariously on a pinnacle of pantisocratic fervour by the breath of his friends' enthusiasm, and then abandoned, stranded and indignant, to climb down by himself, with his conventional, handsome head ringing and re-echoing hollowly for the rest of his life, so that against his will, even in late Keswick years, the author of the *Vision of Judgment* was still progressive in theory, was still, for instance, making faint democratic gestures in the shape of reducing the tendency of his servants to call him 'sir.'[1]

We think, when we read of Coleridge at this time, of Hazlitt's famous account of a first sight of him. We can understand how to all who knew him then his after life must have seemed a decay. In more than one way he was strangely un-Coleridgean. His confidence[2] was un-Coleridgean. So was the unity which this confidence gave him. 'S.T.C.' is merged in 'Coleridge,' for the only time in his life. The unworldliness which was later to become a vice stultifying action is now a godlike attribute superbly over-riding the impediment of practical difficulty. With powerful *naïveté* he makes impossible difficulties seem advantages. He is in London to arrange a site for the pantisocrats. He meets a 'most intelligent young man who has spent the last five years of his life in America—and has lately come from thence as an agent to sell land. . . . He recommends the Susquehannah from its excessive Beauty, and its security from hostile Indians,' he says 'that literary characters make *money* there. . . .'[3] If

[1] W. H.
[2] From 1794: I came home at one o'clock this morning in the honest consciousness of having exhibited closer argument in more elegant and appropriate language than I had ever conceived myself capable of. (550)
[3] 545.

Coleridge had had the advantage, the very day before, of reading Dickens' description of Agent Scadder of the Eden Settlement Company, he would still have been magnificently un-knowing enough not to see difficulties about this gentleman.

Un-Coleridgean, also, is his indifference to religion —for the only time in his life he is airy-common-sensical on the subject, in the worst manner of his contemporaries. He does not believe in the Redemption, because it is irrational: he is a Unitarian, because the fact that three equals one is against reason. The point is crucial. Now alone is he indifferent to religion, because he possesses it. Because he was complete in action, and did not need it. Because he was incomplete in consciousness, and could not know it. As Coleridge wrote twenty years later:

> O! never can I remember those days with either shame or regret. For I was most sincere, most disinterested! My opinions were indeed in many and most important points erroneous; but my heart was single. (237)

*

When did this first spring of youth begin to lose its force, or change its quality?

Pantisocracy died down. But other activities came to take its place. Much business, of a negative kind— esteceanism makes its first damaging appearance in the side-steppings, the quarrels, the head-in-sand buryings, the Schillerian posturings connected with Coleridge's marriage. Nevertheless the youthful impetus remains unchecked. There is the same powerful innocence in the Bristol life, the lectures, the *Conciones ad Populum*—even if almost inarticulate; and then the *Watchman*, not so inexpressive, particularly in the *Prospectus*,[1] where this First Idea of Coleridge is formulated more explicitly ('A PEOPLE ARE FREE IN PROPORTION AS THEY FORM THEIR OWN OPINIONS'), where Coleridge is more obviously possessed of some kind of knowledge which makes Godwinism irrelevant. ('Without previous illumination a change in the *forms* of Government will be of no avail.') The youthful power is still there: is obvious from the accounts of his tour as agent for his own *Watchman*, just as it is apparent through the cheerful solemnities of *Conciones*. The interests of his life are extended, even, by a new absorption in dogma, and notional schemes. A great part of his exuberance begins to go to the mastering and the enthusiastic vindication of the metaphysical doctrines then accessible. A theory stage is regular in the evolution of genius. There is no danger, in the case of a Coleridge, of the first eagerly comprehended theory becoming 'ever after fetish.' It is the happy tuning up of the great instrument of thought, preparatory to its creative harmony with action. Locke—Berkeley—Leibnitz it goes. Then Hartley. In 1794 he is telling Southey that he believes 'in the corporeality of thought, namely, that it is motion.' Super Hartleian. 'I am a complete necessitarean.' Metaphysics to Coleridge at this time is a branch of mental exercise, a game, a wit sharpener 'without

[1] Reprinted, 143.

33

which no man *can* reason but with women and children.'[1]

The verb 'to reason,' the act of thinking, was to have a very different significance for Coleridge later. At this time there is too much activity in Coleridge's life for the action of thought to have room. So far, none of the fearful processes of consciousness. Much talking *about* philosophy, many conversions and re-conversions; but no metaphysic of his own, except the grand generalisation, arising from good health, good spirits, and a general sense of power:

> There is one Mind, one omnipresent Mind
> Omnific

or

> All-conscious Presence of the Universe,
> Nature's vast ever-acting Energy!

Typical lines from Coleridge's two long, grave, truly youthful metaphysical poems, clear enough in their words, but not yet articulate beyond the level of the kind of metaphysic he was using as brain-conditioner. Coleridge had come to life. The power to speak of this life came later.

*

1796 is a fair year to quote for a first change, a first development, in Coleridge. In 1796, force and certainty lapse a little. There is a doubt. The feeling of unity in his universe is replaced by a desire to demonstrate that unity. He becomes aware that the fascinating metaphysics and gymnast doctrines which

[1] 550.

were to him 'thought' at this time were strangely unconnected with the life and experience of which he was beginning to be conscious.

So far he had felt no necessity to connect philosophy with experience. He could express a strong deistic sense of God in *Religious Musings* and impregnate other parts of the same poem with mechanically necessitarian doctrines. Early in 1796, believing his wife to have miscarried, he refers to the 'Thing which might have been a Newton or an Hartley'—Hartley at his most materialist, Newton at his most mechanist, is his idea of greatness. Later, in September, when the child is born, it is still called Hartley, but it is in the hope that 'his head will be convinced of, and his heart saturated with, the truths so ably supported by that great master of *Christian* Philosophy. . . .' Coleridge's concept of religion has changed; it begins to represent, vaguely, something which is better than the philosophy he was about to question; he is referring to the second part of Hartley's treatise, an exposition of religion in which the faith its author's materialist doctrines have destroyed is defended.[1]

Something had already happened in Coleridge to make him scornful of the too easy 'explanations' of Hartley's once-fascinating theory of sensations. In *The Destiny of Nations* of this year are first signs of discontent with mechanist philosophy; the first realisation, also (there are certain new depths in the lines which precede this passage), that philosophy can be something more than a fitting together of consistent theories:

[1] *Cf.* J.H.M., 42.

But some . . .
Chain down the wingèd thought, scoffing ascent,
Proud in their meanness: and themselves they cheat
With noisy emptiness of learnèd phrase,
Their subtle fluids. (*P.*, 132)

This is the only year in his life when to Coleridge
metaphysics seem trivial. Knowing only this one kind
of philosophy, he asks the familiar question, proper
to this point in his development: Is philosophy so
important? 'Our quaint metaphysical opinions in an
hour of anguish like playthings by the bedside of a
child deadly sick,' he notes. For the first time, what
philosophy can be is beginning to dawn on him. He
wonders whether Dr. Priestley is satisfied with his
'eating, drinking, lustful God with no unity of Consciousness'[1] . . . has Dr. Priestley forgotten 'that In-
comprehensibility is as necessary an attribute of the
First Cause as Love, or Poems . . .'? He is surprised
that Dr. Darwin 'seems all at once to make up his
mind on such important subjects as whether we be
the outcasts of a blind idiot called Nature, or the
children of an all-wise and infinitely good God.'[2]
Coleridge is beginning to realise, as if for the first
time, what 'opinions' can mean.

The outward signs of change are not at first very
promising. He repeats, and is proud of, the phrase
about his having broken his squeaking baby-trumpet
of sedition. Says that he is 'wearied to soreness' of
politics. More seriously, he is 'library cormorant' once

[1] 561. [2] *L.*, 153.

more—untried neoplatonists, new travel books. Half-seriously, on the eve of going to Stowey, he is determined to lead a new kind of *practical* life—'I *will* be (please God) an horticulturalist and a farmer.'[1]

Meagre prophecies of the sudden and famous new experience which Coleridge was about to incorporate into his life at this time. Famous because it is so clearly reflected by the change in his poetry.

*

As a writer, Coleridge had never been precocious. Struggling to conform with certain styles, rather than to transcend them, he had allowed remarkably little of his own meaning to pass over to the reader. In his Cambridge days, for instance, Coleridge had been fond of writing about Nature, communing with it in an eighteenth-century manner which Cowper and Crabbe, which even Dr. Johnson, had long derided.[2] Farcical eighteenth-century gravities asserting that hamlets are peaceful, rustics pensive, and the wood-nymph solitude sad. In 1795–6 there are signs of a change. A year or two later there is a complete metamorphosis. Articulation, in earlier poems confined to an occasional beautiful expression of an abstract thought, becomes general. Coleridge now wants to describe what he has seen of the slow oozing tears of coloured lichens, or pools, among rocks, scarce wrinkled by the blast; and developing from this comes the true nature poetry of *The Ancient Mariner*, or the closing lines of *Frost at Midnight*. Rather suddenly, the verse has become

[1] 566.   [2] *P.*, 58.

poetical verse; and what this change implies, the new notebooks demonstrate. Coleridge is changing from a man of notions, ideals, metaphysics, and merely Wertheran introspection to a man of joy in detail, pleasure in external fact, in shape of a cloud, in quality of moonlight: Coleridge, who Hamletised his way through so much of his life, is finding his subjective world restored to efficacy by reviving draughts from outside, is aware of circles of light on a mountain, of the texture of wood-flame: is more than observant, in the company of new friends, of last red leaves on early winter trees, now seeming to him strangely more beautiful than buds of early spring whose 'vernal airs' he had praised when he was writing what he thought was poetry a few years before.

What had happened to cause this change?

There are certain external changes, which correspond. There was his marriage, and his early happy acquiescence in it, and the birth of his son: all helping to re-connect him with life.

More important, there were new relationships with Poole and the Wordsworths—friends who were different from Lamb, who were in every way to be contrasted with Southey.[1] Coleridge found for the first time friends who fundamentally agreed with him, not in the sense of sharing similar opinions, but in the sense that their life and aims were level with his own, equal in depths and purpose. In some sense, this new Coleridge grew from these new contacts.

Nevertheless the change came from Coleridge him-

[1] The different significance of these friendships is outlined on p. 162 ff.

self; or rather it is part of that event in the explanation of which the phrases 'from outside,' 'from inside,' have least validity. The new poetry is the direct outcome of an increase in experience. Coleridge himself had enlarged himself, by the experience from nature.

*

From the first, even before its results show, he was able to describe the experience itself. When the sun sets, kindling the blue ocean, he stands 'struck with deep joy. . . . Silent with swimming sense . . . gazing till all doth seem less gross than bodily. . . .' Or, at another time, it seems to him that he is aware of something more akin to a process than to a sudden exaltation. The exchange between himself and the outside world is something gradual:

> And after lonely sojourning
> In such a quiet and surrounded nook,
> This burst of prospect, here the shadowy main,
> Dim-tinted, there the mighty majesty
> Of that huge amphitheatre of rich
> And elmy fields, seems like society—
> Conversing with the mind, and giving it
> A livelier impulse and a dance of thought!

But for Coleridge it is not enough to describe. He wants to en-Coleridge the experience by knowing it. He begins to try to make it conscious.

First, he philosophises on it, Platonically. Nature, he affirms, is not important: it is a symbol of what lies behind. It is a 'mighty alphabet for infant minds,' and we in this low world are 'Placed with our backs to bright Reality, That we may learn with young unwounded ken. . . .'[1] A year later (1797) he is inclined to retire to the heights of Contemplation, making his character, Osorio, say:

> It were a lot divine in some small skiff
> Along some Ocean's boundless solitude,
> To float for ever with a careless course,
> And think myself the only being alive! (134)

At the same time he feels the insufficiency of this. He regrets the temptation to float, like the Indian Vishnu, 'along an infinite ocean cradled in the flower of the Lotus.' He feels that the experience should find expression in action. But what action?

It has made him happy. It must, through him, make others happy also. 'I love fields and woods and mountains,' he says, writing to the Rev. George Coleridge, always anxious to know what his younger brother is actually engaged in, 'with an almost visionary fondness.'

> And because I have found benevolence and quietness growing within me as that fondness has increased, therefore I should wish to be the means of implanting it in others. (576)

In verse he maintains that he has found 'Religious meanings in the forms of nature. . . .'

It is a truth which Coleridge has only half earned the right to speak. So far, Coleridge can only general-

[1] *P.*, 132.

ise, half mature. New truths were in the air, but he had not yet 'by meditation made them part of his feelings.'

*

The years of Coleridge's attainment of self-knowledge are 1799, 1800, 1801. Important instruments in this attainment are Spinoza, and certain German philosophers. One way of referring to this period is to say: Then (unhappily) did Coleridge come under the influence of the German transcendentalists.

He did indeed. He alone of the Englishmen of his age was able to guess, partly by hearsay, but more by intuition and the fact of his ripeness in experience, that the new philosophers in Germany would help him to know himself and to realise this experience. Before he went he seems only to have known the romantics—Schiller especially—at first hand. In 1796 he refers to the 'most unintelligible Immanuel Kant.' During his actual visit he seemed to spend his time learning the language and attending scientific and philological lectures. But as a result of going to Germany he collected for his future study, he found because he wanted to find, the work of writers involved in the same problems as himself; and he wanted to find these writers because, before he went, he was conscious of unassimilated change and development. Writing in *Biographia* of 1798, he says that he felt in that year that 'a more thorough revolution in my philosophical principles, and a deeper insight into my heart, were still wanting.' Writing before the event, he says: 'I look upon the realisation of the German scheme as of great importance to my intellectual activity, and, of course, to my moral happiness.' And he furiously annoyed Charles Lamb by his way of promising, when he came back, intellectual refreshment for the uninitiate. All the sighs over the 'pity of Coleridge having taken to German metaphysics' are wasted breath. If only he could have summoned up worldly tact enough to say in the *Biographia* what he made so clear in letters and unread notes, a whole generation of misunderstanding might have been avoided. Talking, in 1825, about the 'mistaken notion of my German metaphysics' he utters a controversy-cancelling truth, a statement of developing, as opposed to converted, opinion:

> 'All the elements, the *differentials*, as the algebraists say, of my present opinions existed for me before I had ever seen a book of German Metaphysics, later than Wolf and Leibnitz, or could have read it, if I had.'

'Differentials' is the right word. German Metaphysics accelerated the development of seeds of differentiation that were already in Coleridge. His use of Kant and Schelling is not a loss of individuality, but an intensification of it.

For a time, the thirty volumes that Coleridge brought back from Germany remained unread. The first smell of German philosophy turned him to the re-reading of Spinoza. '98 and '99 are Coleridge's Spinoza years, representing for Coleridge a maturation stage between the adopted philosophies of his mid-twenties and the personal metaphysic beginning to evolve in 1800. It is likely that Spinoza clarified Coleridge more than any one German. 'Strong feeling and an active intellect combined, lead almost necessarily, in the first stage of philosophising, to Spinosism.'[1] He was reading with absolute absorption, en-Coleridgising. 'Sunk in Spinoza,' amid the family distractions of a too-small house, 'as undisturbed as a Toad in a Rock.'[2] But it was not long before Kant took hold of him—'with giant hands.' Now was philosophy made to appear a new kind of subject, more than interesting, never plausible, less comprehensible, at first glance, and therefore a closer metaphor of truth than, say, the analogies of Hume. Coleridge found himself *concerned* in the subject as never before when he discovered in Kant's distinction between reason and understanding what seemed to him a more radical statement of his own newly evolved distinction between fancy and the imagination.

The first impact of the discovery of this new world of philosophy moved Coleridge to disentangle himself meticulously from the schools in which he had been raised. No room in Hume or Hartley for such mysteries as those sunset feelings when he stood at Stowey 'silent with swimming sense.' But to the world of Kant, it seemed, these things were native. Coleridge felt he was discovering philosophy for the first time. By 1800 he is becoming finally impatient of the whole atmosphere of materialism. He does not like Miss Hayes, for instance.

[1] 414.   [2] *U.L.*, i. 126.

Of Miss Hayes' intellect I do not think so highly as you, or rather, to speak sincerely, I think not *contemptuously* but certainly *despectively* thereof. Yet I think you likely in this case to have judged better than I; for to hear a thing, ugly and petticoated, ex-syllogize a God with cold-blooded precision, and attempt to run religion through the body with an icicle, an icicle from a Scotch Hog-trough! I do not endure it; my eye beholds phantoms, and 'nothing is, but what is not.' (*L.*, 232)

He does not like common-sense refutations of God. He begins to distinguish the 'mechanic' and the 'transcendental' philosophy. He writes crucial letters to Poole:

If I do not greatly delude myself, I have not only *completely extricated the notions of time and space*, but have overthrown the doctrine of association, as taught by Hartley, and with it all the irreligious metaphysics of modern infidels—especially the doctrine of necessity. . . . *I write this to you only, and I pray you, mention what I have written to no one.* (588)

*

Newton was a mere materialist. *Mind*, in his system, is always *passive,*—a lazy *looker-on* at an external world. . . .

My opinion is thus: that deep thinking is attainable only by a man of deep feeling, and that all truth is a species of revelation.

. . . I need not observe, my dear friend, how unutterably silly and contemptible these opinions would be if written to any but to another self. (590)

The seriousness, the expressed belief, in the first letter, that he is dealing with truths 'the importance of which came to him almost as a revelation,' and— true Coleridgean sign—the desire to act in association with a friend, all show that these are not mere conversions of opinion; that Coleridge himself is changing. Nor is 'change' the right word. Coleridge had always had an ear for certain non-mechanist writers, in spite of his early fascinated adherence to explainers like Hartley, and his common-sense patronage of mystical philosophy.[1] In a neglected chapter of *Biographia* he talks of his continual return, during his ideological period, to the writings of George Fox and Jacob Behmen:

> For the writings of these mystics acted in no slight degree to prevent my mind from being imprisoned within the outline of any single dogmatic system. They contributed to keep alive the *heart* in the *head*; gave me an indistinct, yet stirring and working presentiment, that all the produce of the mere *reflective* faculty partook of DEATH, and were as the rattling twigs and sprays in winter, to which a sap was yet to be propelled from some root to which I had not penetrated.

The differentials had always been there. There was no 'conversion to German transcendentalism.' Coleridge, in the metamorphosis to *imago*, is changing his food. Articulate at last, Coleridge's own philosophy begins to appear.

Coleridge now was able to know the experience

---

[1] 'I love Plato, his dear, *gorgeous* nonsense.' (*L.*, 211)

from nature deeply enough to relate it to the rest of his life—to have a philosophy as large as the creative pleasures of Stowey. With this inception of his philosophy is associated the word 'imagination.'

It was while he was listening, he says, to a poem of Wordsworth's, and appreciating in it an excellence which he 'no sooner felt than sought to understand,' that he was first impelled to put into words what he was beginning to recognise as a new faculty, then described for the first time as 'imagination.' This was at Stowey. But the realisation of the active meaning of the word, and its full acclimatisation into his world, was the result of this education of his consciousness which followed. Contemplation and the Indian Vishnu he had already found unsatisfactory—the side-stepping of experience. Now, in its turn, the mere active delight in externals of nature, with isolated moments of objective apprehension, seems incomplete. He makes a note, at this time, of a quarrel with Wordsworth and Hazlitt, whom he has reproved for speaking malignantly of the 'Divine wisdom.' Wordsworth had been ruthless on the subject of the pettifications of dogmatists and creed men. He accuses Wordsworth, in effect, of being a pedant in the cause of Joy in Nature, carrying consciousness of God no further than Pantheism: 'Surely, always to be looking at the superficies of objects for the purpose of taking delight in their beauty, and sympathy with their real or imagined life, is as deleterious to the health and manhood of the intellect as always to be peering and unravelling'[1]

[1] 162.

(Wordsworth's point against religiosity). 'Joy in outward objects' at any rate seemed inadequate to
describe the creative impulses which had given birth
to the poems. Now at last he was able to describe
this faculty more relevantly. Now, instead of a Bowles
of rural gentilities, or a metaphysically ingenious
Hartley, his prototype of the Complete Man is a
Wordsworth whom he sees as

> the only man who has effected a complete and
> constant synthesis of thought and feeling and com-
> bined them with poetic forms, with the music of
> pleasurable passion, and with Imagination or the
> *modifying* power in that highest sense of the word,
> in which I have ventured to oppose it to Fancy, or
> the *aggregating* power—in that sense in which it is a
> dim analogue of creation—not all that we can *believe*,
> but all that we can *conceive* of creation. (612)

Embryonic to the lucidity of 1825, perhaps, but a
very different kind of consciousness from that of the
Bristol Coleridge, enthusiastically discovering vibratiuncle theories. Now has 'philosophy,' now has
'thought' for Coleridge changed indeed. Thought is
no longer a rounding off of the old, but a generation
of the new. Something more akin to a feeling, when
'feeling' means not a sensation merely, nor an intuition, but a kind of knowing comparable to that
by which an acorn becomes an oak. Now begins his
conception of philosophy as the bringing of this
secondary, deeper knowledge to consciousness. It is
possible, now, to understand what Humphry Davy

47

means when he prophesies that his friend is to identify himself with the 'philosophy of feeling.'

> Believe me, Southey! a metaphysical solution, that does not instantly *tell* you something in the heart is grievously to be suspected as apocryphal. I almost think that ideas *never* recall ideas, as far as they are ideas, any more than leaves in a forest create each other's motion. The breeze it is that runs through them—it is the soul, the state of feeling. (*L.*, 428)

This time of Coleridge's life, just after the turn of the century, is a kind of apex of his development. He had still the appetite for effective action which has been described as his powers of youth: at the same time there was more advantageous leverage to this action by reason of the fact that it was more deeply grounded in self-knowledge. Now, before it grows cold in the shadow of tragedy, a last look at this youth of Coleridge.

'There are moments when I have such a power of life in me,'[1] he can write at the end of 1799. There is his old life-and-death intensity about the move to the lakes, and his delight in the new surroundings, and in what seems the perfection and miraculous convenience of everything, and the splendid nearness of the Wordsworths. All the preparation to turn into a practical farmer when he moved to Stowey has its homomorph at Keswick in the decision to become a practical scientist. As contact to stimulate this life-long interest to special intensity Humphry Davy

[1] 580.

seems to have been brought in. In the first year of Keswick, Coleridge is Baconian. His hands are scratched—by a cat from whose back he was trying to comb sparks in order to see whether the light from them was refrangible by a prism. Davy is deluged with questions—'What is the cause of that sense of cold, which accompanies inhalation, after having eaten peppermint drops? . . . How is this explained in philosophical language divested of corpuscular theories?' Scientific words creep into the descriptions of the letters: 'the air that yonder sallow-faced and yawning Tourist is breathing is to my Babe a perpetual Nitrous Oxide.' And Davy must have been made conscious of the responsibilities of a friendship with Coleridge when he received requests like these:

> I beg you, therefore, my dear Davy, to write me a long letter when you are at leisure, informing me: Firstly, What books it will be well for me and Calvert to purchase. Secondly, Directions for a convenient little laboratory. Thirdly, To what amount apparatus would run in expense, and whether or no you would be so good as to superintend its making at Bristol. Fourthly, Give me your advice how to *begin*. (588)

This is exactly the Coleridge of the early seventeen-nineties. Again the typical, suddenly developed appetite for a new kind of activity, again the earliest stages in its satisfaction seeming to give him the objective restoration, the re-connection with the external world he needed. The difference is that besides the powers

49

of doing, and the old eloquence to exalt them, there are the new powers of knowing as well. Coleridge's philosophy of identity is emerging because he is successfully following the endless process of self-completion. In 1802 he writes these lines of advice to a young poet:

> Poetic feelings, like the stretching boughs
> Of mighty oaks, pay homage to the gales,
> Toss in the strong winds, drive before the gust,
> Themselves one giddy storm of fluttering leaves;
> Yet, all the while, self-limited remain
> Equally near the fixed and solid trunk
> Of Truth and Nature in the howling storm,
> As in the calm that stills the aspen grove.   (*P.*, 375)

Coleridge now is complete, with the never-satisfied completeness of a tree: once again he is standing, as the evolving man always stands, on the threshold.

*

Coleridge never crossed this new threshold. An impediment, mysterious and immaterial, lay in his way. Years later, wounded in body, mind, and soul, he was able to drag himself back—but it was not a Coleridge capable of further evolution.

The nature of the impediment becomes clear, I think, in the description of its effects.

The first sign is a change, not in itself necessarily retrograde. Coleridge gradually ceases to 'see' the external world. The experience from nature, and its reflection in his verse, ceases.

Coleridge's farewell to this part of his life is set forth in famous verses of the *Ode to Dejection*.

And those thin clouds above, in flakes and bars,
That give away their motion to the stars;
Those stars, that glide behind them or between,
Now sparkling, now bedimmed, but always seen:
Yon crescent Moon, as fixed as if it grew
In its own cloudless, starless lake of blue,
I see them all so excellently fair,
I see, not feel, how beautiful they are!

However much the beauty of the words may belie the thought, this special faculty was truly in decay. 'The poet in me is dead,' he says.

My imagination (or rather the Somewhat that had been imaginative) lies like a cold snuff on the circular rim of a brass candlestick, without even a stink of tallow to remind you that it was once clothed and mitred with flame. That is past by! (591)

Coleridge means many things by poet, but in the sense in which he is using the word here, it is true. In spite of later premonitions that the spirit of poetry was again stirring in him, objectivity fades from his writing so completely that in a few years he can tritely assert, as if he had lapsed back to the eighteenth-century manner of his youth, as if he had never been 'struck silent with swimming sense' in his life, that he is essaying to

> trace in leaves and flowers that round me lie
> Lessons of love and earnest piety. . . .   (*P.*, 429)

Far, indeed, from the experience from nature.

But there are other experiences, perhaps, not less important, of which Coleridge was capable. Why, instead of nostalgic yearnings after a former condition, does he not pass to a new one?

Coleridge himself gives a reason, dogmatically.

> *Now afflictions bow me down to earth.*

He does not specify the afflictions in his poem, but he is not silent about them in his letters. Bad health is one of them. But the prime impediment he affirms to be his unsuccessful marriage. After 1800, or earlier, Mrs. Coleridge, brought up to regard marriage as an affair of economics, and convinced that from this point of view she had been hopelessly unhappy in her husband, hardened her attitude towards him into one of constant 'dyspathy' (Coleridge's word), and petty thwarting. This, Coleridge convinced himself, was the major affliction.

A torture, certainly, not the less severe because petty. But Coleridge had changed the environment of his life before: and sorrows are sorrows, and Coleridge was more fit than most to thrive on such. Joys indeed impregnate, but sorrows bring forth: and for a time Coleridge seemed to be not only retaining but sharpening his integrity by keeping his troubles boldly within the field of his consciousness. The *Ode* itself is evidence. The letters, in which the *Ode* is very frequently quoted, confirm. He tries to make himself more fully aware, too, of his physical, besides his marital, ill-health. He tries to know what pain is, to 'look it fully in the face,' he says. And, as abecedarian in the technique of husbandhood as he is expert in the technique of the soul, he tries to tell not only himself but his wife where the causes of their quarrel lie, in what points they are regrettably different, how she is inferior, with a thirdly, fourthly, fifthly. Coleridge is struggling to keep step with unhappiness.

But every source of that unhappiness is growing. His fear, that he will lose his integrity, becomes more and more urgent—the fear, as he puts it, that 'each visitation . . . suspends . . . my shaping spirit of Imagination. . . .'

Coleridge's fears were well founded. Coleridge, knowing himself, knew his future.

Avoid—forget. Coleridge follows the well-beaten path of tragedy. But not yet quite engulfed: still conscious, even of the machinery of avoidance. He forms a plan, he says, not to think of what he needs must feel. He tries to bring about artificial divergence of fact and feeling by taking refuge in 'abstruse research': 'In my long illness,' he writes, 'I had compelled into hours of delight many a sleepless, painful hour of darkness by chasing down metaphysical game. . . .' And then an expressive description of intellectual activity pursued for its own sake, of thinking forced beyond knowledge, thinking which found no answer 'in the heart':

I have continued the hunt, till I found myself unaware at the root of Pure Mathematics—and up the tall, smooth tree, whose few poor branches are all at its very summit, am I climbing by pure adhesive strength of arms and thighs, still slipping down, still renewing my ascent. (591)

Later, as 'Coleridge' becomes obscured, the self-deception becomes more complete. In 1804, after two years of indecision, Coleridge went to Malta. His official reason, health : his own private reason, 'a holiday from domestic infelicity.' The real reason—Coleridge wanted to 'go to Moscow' (to make from the *Three Sisters* a name for the topographical fallacy). Coleridge caught at the delusion that it was possible to escape a personal crisis by changing its site.

In fact, the years from 1804 to 1808—Malta, and after the return—are the most terrifyingly obscure years of his life. One thing is certain, that they were years of misery; unfruitful, negative misery, beyond Coleridge's powers of experience: years, indeed, when 'Coleridge' scarcely existed, and obscure because not only the powers of consciousness, but the instinct to record, were almost eclipsed. Especially ruinous because when 'Coleridge' lapsed, the 'S.T.C.' which took his place was so entirely unsuited to the tiding over of black days, so uncompromisingly innocent of the kind of fortitude advocated by bedside mottoes.

On his return the adverse fate seems to him more insuperable than ever. All is altered. Where previously had been flexible relationships with the problems and men of his world, stagnating 'situations' developed.

He was thrown back on the Wordsworths, for instance
—old centres of strength for him. But now, while
their side of it was all hospitality and protection, and
pity, Coleridge found himself in no sort of formative
contact with them. He yielded to the presence of
Wordsworth, finding comfort in the strong character,
and luxuriating in the pain of contrasting his own fate
with that of one who had encountered the domestic side
of life with dignity and success—'adored by two, and
two such beings . . .' Coleridge indulged in jealousy.
'O mercy—' God have mercy, Coleridge cries.[1]

The situation with his wife was equally static or
disintegrating. I have lately had to try to understand
this part of Coleridge's life and describe it in the
preparation of another book. One fact soon became
clear: that though of course the marriage was in no
sense the cause of Coleridge's tragedy, his behaviour
when it had already become a demonstrable failure
embodies all its elements.

Before they had been married a year, Mrs. Coleridge
had become an anachronism. She was a product of
the Idealist period, chosen enthusiastically, but impersonally, as a Mate suitable for rearing infant
Pantisocrats, and married, less enthusiastically, when
the Pantisocratic theme was dead and was replaced by
a consanguineous sense of honour (the 'merest phan-
tom of overstrained honour,' it was to be called later).
It is true that for a year or two the social and physical
novelties of the situation kept him happy—but it is
one thing to choose friends during an idealist phase:

if necessary it is possible, when a closer concentration on the Object brings its surprises, to stand aloof, like rocks which have been rent asunder, the scars remaining: but the standing aloof is much more difficult in the case of the *wife* whom the husband has been unlucky enough to marry at a period when all seemed equal in the sight of the radiant, half-uplifted, idealist eye. At any other period of his life Coleridge would have been able to see that Sarah was the least suitable of wives for him. A companion of similar tastes need not have been essential: nor perhaps could he hope for the chance in a thousand—the self-contained individual with a rich world of her own to exchange.[1] But an affectionate bosom such a man does need, a loving and above all a reverencing bosom, as Wordsworth his Mary's, or Southey his Edith's. Mrs. Coleridge had no world of her own, only a suburb, received at fourth hand from the standards of Bristol respectability. Moreover, she was quite unable to recognise, much less to respect, the gods of her husband. His books did not sell. There was no more to be said. No sane person who had lived in the Keswick household could have seriously compared the importance of art or the elucidation of the human soul with the importance of getting money or begetting children. Those who have glanced through Mrs. Coleridge's letters will recognise what I mean. Mr. Dawe, the artist, is staying at Keswick. The house is full of children. Mrs. Southey is on the verge of her seventh accouchement. 'When the boys go,' writes Mrs. Coleridge, 'we hope Mr. D.

[1] Cf. A.T.T., pp. 26-end.

will also return to Town, for he is painting a great Picture in C.'s Study, subject, A Woman on the point of a high Rock, taking her infant from an Eagle's Nest; the Eagle flying over her head—and this painting business creates a great deal of bustle—and running *in and out*, windows open to paint the scenery, etc., etc. —which we can well dispense with in her confinement . . .'[1] I gather from the *D.N.B.* that Mr. Dawe became R.A. on the strength of this picture.

Notwithstanding the line taken by the Royal Academy, the world will sympathise with Mrs. Coleridge. But—what should Coleridge have done? Coleridge, who to his relatives was less effectively 'artistic' even than Mr. Dawe? We know how a 'strong character' would act in such a situation. He would batter down the obstacles, and win heroically through, hardened and blunted perhaps, but with self-respect intact. Earlier, I compared Coleridge, his ramifications impetuously diversified yet united at the root, with a tree. We know how a tree would behave. If a sapling meets some obstacle in its course, with the lightest possible heart, and the most cheerful innocence of questions of honour, self-respect, propriety, it turns aside. It alters the direction of its growth. Thus, a few years earlier, might Coleridge have acted. Thus, with the aid of some surface dressing of disapproval, did he turn aside from Southey. Thus should he have left his wife.

He could not so act now. He seemed to stand aside, with the vicious misery of might-have-been-ism, watch-

[1] S.P., 19.

ing his fate; his antipathy to his wife, his admiration of the Wordsworths, his love for Sarah Hutchinson, whom he had turned into the fatal embodiment of his wife as she might have been—all were inactive. But the real calamity was no celestial fate. It was the fact that Coleridge had lost his capacity for naïve experience, had refused to acknowledge changes in himself, urgent for expression. As Dorothy Wordsworth was to say later, he could no longer act from simplicity. The castigation which he should have reserved as a spur to himself became a form of self-indulgence when it was directed against the weakness of his external character. So the situation dragged on, Coleridge vanishing, turning up again. Complaining unmanfully and ungenerously to comparative strangers. Laying the whole case before brother George. In an agony of regret for having laid the whole case before brother George. Agonies of regrets.

> . . . there is a period in a man's life, varying in various men, from thirty-five to forty-five, and operating most strongly in bachelors, widowers, or those worst and miserablest widowers, unhappy husbands, in which a man finds himself at the *top of the hill*, and having attained, perhaps, what he wishes, begins to ask himself, What is all this for?—begins to feel the vanity of his pursuits, becomes half-melancholy, gives in to wild dissipation or self-regardless drinking. (181)

Coleridge was congealing—a process not unpleasant to the poor in spirit: but for a man who has once touched life . . . He is articulate even here. There is some kind of disjointed record of growth quenched against unassimilable sorrow, growth turned back on itself into a process of death. It was at Malta, away from his friends, that he seemed to have felt most the 'Sense of past Youth, and Manhood come in vain.' Capable of happiness, he is capable of despair as well. *I do not know what it is to have one happy moment, or one genial feeling. Not one, so help me God! No visitation of mind in fancy, but only the same dull gnawing pain at the heart. . . .*[1]

Coleridge had come to feel that recovery was impossible. The 'grave-stone had entered into his heart.' His life seemed uncontrollably sinking from him, the flood of its past richness made all the more clear to the onlookers by the catastrophe of the grotesque carcase, ungainly and denuded, exposed by the ebb. Coleridge despaired, because the cause of his tragedy was *not* an unsuitable marriage, nor bad advice from Southey; because it was *not* due to any famous weakness, nor to physical illness; nor to psychological illness, though there is a study to be written from this point of view.[2] Coleridge despaired because he had refused to follow a new direction of his life. 'Till then,' as he said of this period later, 'my life flowed.' 'Dreadful was the feeling' of the change. Coleridge began to look back with agony to the past, because his present was non-existent.

[1] *U.L.*, i. 333.
[2] The cattle of Coleridge's dreams are waiting to be classified: it would no doubt be illuminating, as *Æsop's Fables* are illuminating.

We all look up to the blue sky for comfort, but nothing appears there, nothing comforts, nothing answers us, and so we die. (188)

*

In 1806, when Coleridge returned, when the carcase was washed up—almost literally—on the shores of England, old admirers, hoping for some kind of recovery, were appalled. The prince of intellectual adventure had become stouter, even the eye was dimmed, and the air of unconscious leadership was replaced by a distressing mixture of humility and self-assertiveness. His friends urged him to exert himself —but when they approached intimacies and cruxes, he who before would have been moved to an eloquence in just such a context, turned aside. Even from Poole:

Let eagle bid the Tortoise sunward soar—
  As vainly strength speaks to a broken Mind.
(*P.*, 498)

Even from the Wordsworths. From 1806 to 1810 Coleridge became more and more ingrained in the habit of despair, incapable of any kind of action except in the most fleeting spasm. At the end of this period, Dorothy describes him. To those who had known the Coleridge of 1800 the description would have been recognisable—*by antithesis*. Every life process has been reversed:

. . . his whole time and thoughts . . . are employed in deceiving himself and seeking to deceive others . . . you feel perpetually new hollowness and emptiness. . . . He lies in bed, always till after 12 o'clock, sometimes much later; and never walks out. Even the finest spring day does not tempt him to seek the fresh air; and this beautiful valley seems a blank to him. . . . Sometimes he does not speak a word; and when he does talk it is always upon subjects as far aloof from himself, or his friends, as possible. (D.S., 248)

We look up to the blue sky for comfort . . nothing appears there. . . . But Coleridge had gone beyond despair.

Coleridge, in fact, needed comfort—and so badly that if he could not find it in the sky he was capable of putting it there himself. He turned to self-deceptions. He turned, for instance, to a comfort religion.

He tried to make a human connection with a subject the superhumanities of which he understood more deeply than any of his contemporaries. The ex-deist, the potential comprehender of mystery, announces his belief in a god with whom communication is possible in no mystical sense,[1] and acquires a creed which included the promise of forgiveness of sins to the repentant. Coleridge in these years was repentant, if he was nothing else. Every trait of S.T.C., all his mannerisms, now standing high and dry above the ebb of the true Coleridge, composed the kind of soil in which repentance, self-flagellation, and self-disgust flourished. S.T.C. writes of the doctrine of Redemption:

God of his goodness grant, that I may arrive at a more living faith in this last, than I now feel. What

[1] *B.L.*, i. xxxi.

I now feel is only a very strong presentiment . . .
(*U.L.*, i. 351)

There was no *now*, for Coleridge: to try to live again
in his own splendid past was torture. Therefore he
placed in his empty sky a comforting future, pleasant
with heavens, where his sins and errors would be
cancelled away by a forgiving Christ.

A different kind of comfort, of longer standing, and
of more inescapable after-effects, was opium. It may
seem strange to have written fifty pages—biographical
of a sort—without a mention of this. But Coleridge
has already suffered too much from our contemporary
'Ah! *T.B.*' or 'Of course, *Œdipus*' kind of diagnosis.
Not only the depths of his degradation, but sometimes
even the heights of his poetic creation as well, have
been accounted for by a diminishing 'Ah! Drugs'
judgment.[1] Yet if it is absurd to discuss opium as a
cause, it is worth a digression as a reflection, of the
evolution of Coleridge.

From schooldays up to 1800, Coleridge took
laudanum because almost everyone took it at one
time or another—*e.g.* men of the highest respect and
solidity, such as Southey. Because it was cheap, easy
to get, and regularly prescribed. Because through
sleeping out all night by the side of a stream when he
was a child, or through trying to exhibit himself as
a swimmer, some kind of rheumatic evil soaked into
his bones to ache its way out later with the kind of
pain which made laudanum seem, to doctors and him-

---

[1] Even J.H.M. (p. 144).

elf, the natural remedy. For this period may be
quoted Gillman's *Life*: 'Half his time from seventeen
to eighteen was passed in the sick-ward of Christ's
Hospital, afflicted with jaundice and rheumatic fever.'
Coleridge himself: 'Opium never used to have any
disagreeable effects on me' (1791): talk of 'sopping
the Cerberus' with opium, 1796: and, writing to the
hyper-respectable George: 'you know how divine that
repose (of laudanum) is.'

Perhaps, in 1795, a hint of self-deception: 'Mrs.
Coleridge dangerously ill. . . . I have been obliged to
take laudanum almost every night.' S.T.C.'s bad
management of mundane detail already begins to
interpose. He is already fumbling ruinously among
the precarious adjustments of his health. The doses
of his medicine are already recklessly large (*cf. U.L.*,
i. 59). But the quantity is not yet great enough to
affect him seriously, and it is taken with a clear
conscience, openly.

Taken, there are even some who suggest, to the
improvement of his verse. The stock instance—*Kubla
Khan*, which was composed in, or as a result of, an
opium sleep. 'In consequence of a slight indisposition,'
Coleridge wrote in his best Preface manner, 'an ano-
dyne had been prescribed. . . .' It is possible that one
poor instrument helping to facilitate the expression
of the great change in Coleridge between 1795 and
1797 may have been a drug: he may have found himself released by it, in the preliminary innocuous phase,
into more daring sincerity, drinking laudanum, as
Captain Shotover drank rum, to keep sober. Re-

member also a later confession, that 'though he could think, he could never write, when he was in pain.'

Coleridge's fall is reflected in the history of the subsequent stages. At Keswick there is rain; and rain, for him, meant painful bad health. Larger doses follow—still as part of a prescription. And then, gradually, more often than the pain demands. In 1802 Coleridge begins to show a fatal lack of consciousness of his actions, using laudanum as a means to ward off the effects not of rheumatism but of laudanum poisoning:

> On my arrival at St. Clears, I received your letter, and had scarcely read it before a fluttering of the heart came on, which ended (as usual) in a sudden and violent diarrhœa. I could scarcely touch my dinner and was obliged at last to take 20 drops of Laudanum which now that I have for 10 days left off all stimulus of all kinds, excepting ⅓rd of a grain of opium at night, acted upon me more powerfully than 80 or 100 drops would have done at Keswick. I slept sound while I did sleep; but I am not *quite* well this morning; but I shall get round again in the course of the day—You must see by this, what absolute necessity I am under of *dieting* myself, and if possible, the still greater importance of *tranquillity* to me. . . . (604)

For an early sign of opium as an escape from self, there is an extraordinary letter to Tom Wedgwood, a dangerous friend for Coleridge from the fact that he was himself at this time trying to make a slow death bearable with the help of varieties of drugs.

Euthanasia was to be a thought probably not very far from Coleridge himself in the near future:

> Last night I received a four-ounce parcel-letter by the Post. . . . I *should* have been indignant, if dear Poole's *Squint* of Indignation had not set me a-laughing. In opening it it contained my letter from Gunville, and a parcel, a small one, of *Bang* from Purkis. . . . We will have a fair trial of *Bang*— do bring down some of the Hyoscyamine Pills, and I will give a fair Trial of Opium, Hensbane, and Nepenthe. By the bye, I always considered Homer's account of the *Nepenthe* as a *Banging* Lie. (*U.L.*, i. 252.)

This letter shows that the self-deception stage had already started. Coleridge would never have been consciously cynical in the face of the moral disapproval of a friend like Poole. It is a symptom of decay. The self-deception, the sanguine plans of his youth had something positive—was not self-deception because it was given validity by his youth. This grandeur now begins to be undermined by small, comic signs of human weakness, perfectly reflected in these opium references. The tongue which mocks genius is cursed, but for truth these sentences must be recorded. In 1802 Coleridge is beginning to force himself into a conviction of the harmlessness of opium:

> I am fully convinced, and so is T. Wedgwood, that to a person with such a stomach and bowels as mine, if any stimulus is needful, opium in the small quantities I now take it is incomparably better in every respect than beer, wine, spirits, or any *fermented*

liquor, nay, far less pernicious than even tea. It *i*
my particular wish that Hartley and Derwent should hav
as little tea as possible, and always very weak, with mor
than half milk. Read this sentence to Mary, and t
Mrs. Wilson. (*L.*, 413)

In 1804 the deception seems studied. Writing to hi
wife, especially, he is inclined to add more deliber
ately hypocritical—almost consciously hypocritical—
touches. From a postscript:

I met G. Burnett the day before yesterday i
Lincoln's Inn Fields, so nervous, so helpless witl
such opium-stupidly-wild eyes.
  Oh, it made the place one calls the heart feel a
it was going to ache. (*L.*, 467)

Once the deception started, it grew to extraordinar
lengths, and was extended to fictitious accounts o
his activities, assertions of work accomplished, etc
As Coleridge confessed later (in 1814): 'I have in thi
one dirty business of Laudanum an hundred time
deceived, tricked, nay, actually and consciously *lied*.'
In this same letter Coleridge tries to estimate th
actual quantities of his worst period: 'At length, i
became too bad. I used to take four to five ounces a
day of Laudanum, once (?) ounces, *i.e.* near a Pint—
besides great quantities of opium.'
  The last stage was as unrestrained as every othe
aspect of Coleridge's life. Without full evidence it can
be guessed that he abandoned himself at Malta, that

[1] 654.

on the protracted sea voyage home the nameless agonies of which he complains were the horrors of enforced disintoxication, and that after returning to England sporadic attempts at cures led to spirit drinking, and the inevitable, the classical, consequence of the 'twofold (alcohol-opium) craving.' In the letters almost all the symptoms of which Coleridge complains, and which he assigns to other causes, are those numerated by Dr. Lewin in his analysis of the late stages of morphia poisoning.[1] As thus

Will power is completely paralysed. . . . The perpetual fight between the necessity for decision and the incapacity for it, as well as the consciousness of inferiority and misery with which the victim is obsessed, cause terrible suffering. Even in his dreams this mental torture is continued, for the happy, delightful past is brought into tormenting comparison with the despair of the present. . . .

In the case of such persons every contact with the higher sentiments, love of the family, good humour, faith, reverence, the beauty of nature and the activities of human life is lost. . . .

And then the organic symptoms:

Sticky sweat is excreted, especially at night, from the whole body or from the head alone; the appearance and personal hygiene are neglected . . . attacks of fever with ague . . . gastric pains, colic, diarrhœa with soreness of the anus . . . disturbances of lachrymation. . . .

[1] In *Phantastica.*

Coleridge answers precisely to the clinical picture. No question, now, of the 'helpful effect of opium on Coleridge's verse.' A certain style, the cause of which we can guess, becomes more frequent in his letters. He himself apologises—they are 'flighty' letters, he says. There is a ghastly facetiousness: he is excitedly waggish.[1] No wonder, that ever since Coleridge returned from Malta, critics and friends have been saying 'Ah, Drugs.'

Yet the point remains, that it is fatally confusing to regard opium as in any sense the cause. Coleridge, as has been said, was unable to face the complex tragedies connected with the failure of his domestic life. He was unable at any rate to follow some change in the direction of his life to which his development had been leading him. It may be that his worry over the miseries of his marriage was a kind of motive hunting for the vast inward uneasiness he felt at some failure to sail along this new direction. If such distressful new branches of life are 'sorrow'—the kind of sorrow, as a modern prophet has said, which is the foundation of life—then the foundation of death is the refusal to follow them. And if those who are able not to hold back are few, if those who can achieve sorrow are few, a Coleridge is capable. Yet Coleridge failed, turning sorrow into tragedy, even if it was not a final failure.

And the agent of this avoidance happened to be opium. It might have been any vice—living in accord-

---

[1] *Cf.* for example, *U.L.*, ii. 115.

ance with a rigid, responsibility-avoiding morality: or
blind hard work. But Coleridge chose (very typical,
here, of S.T.C.) the most vicious-seeming and conventionally reprehensible of all the vices; the worst,
the least attractive, in the world's eye.

*

'Begin to count my life, as a Friend of yours,
from . . .'—When? Did Coleridge recover? In what
year, and in what sense did he recover? Coleridge
came near to all kinds of death. Was his superhumanity restored to him? Or his humanity only?
Or did his life, like Wordsworth's, become merely
functional?

The great event of these days was the quarrel with
Wordsworth. Wordsworth's impatient complaint, as
repeated by Montague (that his friend had become a
'perfect nuisance' in the house, was 'rotting his intes-
tines with drink,' etc.—I will not repeat the often-
told story) was the inevitable climax to the clogging
of the once so fluid exchange between them. It was
more than possible that the explosive agonies of this
quarrel may have been a help: it is possible even
that some instinct of self-preservation in Coleridge
made him create this particular shock to this end.
It is certain that he was released by it from a district
whose beauties now meant nothing to him but which
was saturated with destructively sweet reminiscences.
It is obvious that it made possible new concrete friendships of the kind by which he lived.

But the indirect help given by the Wordsworth

break was not enough in itself. In so far as Coleridge recovered, it was because he never quite cut himself off. He never completely lost the thread of his life, worn and whittled as it had become. Even at his worst there was still something in him able to know what was happening—able even to describe. He could describe even those sensations which most urgently demanded forgetfulness. Read the letters of these worst years, and the descriptive power with which he writes down the drug effects seems not so utterly disconnected from the faculty by which he 'knew' purple heath-flowers, and frost at midnight. When the after-effects merged into the new craving: 'the direful moment . . . when my pulse began to fluctuate, my heart to palpitate, and such a dreadful *falling abroad*, as it were, of my whole frame, such intolerable Restlessness and incipient Bewilderment. . . .'[1] 'Falling abroad' is memorable. He was still interested—still curious, at moments, about the wherefore of this strange dis-severing of volition from will, taking the drug, as he did, with full knowledge of its evil. 'But tho' there was no prospect, no gleam of Light before, an indefinite indescribable Terror as with a scourge of ever restless, ever coiling and uncoiling serpents, drove me on from behind.'[2]

A first sign of grace was an effort to confide this real cause of his bad health—a step which took the typical form of a delegation of responsibility to the firmer character of a dependable friend: the move to 'put himself under the charge of some physician.'

[1] 657.   [2] 653.

'Begin to count my life, as a Friend of yours, from 1st January, 1809,'[1] he writes to Poole. He goes on to explain that he has submitted his case, carefully and faithfully, to a physician. 'Such is the blessedness of walking altogether in the light, that my health and spirits are better than I have known them for years.' This was one of many attempts. There were continual set-backs. Panic appeals for help are regular in advanced cases of morphia poisoning. But the reform comes from something deeper than the good resolutions of weakness. Neither his indulgence, nor his recovery, were entirely automatic. Agonised cries of guilt are still frequent:[2] ' "I gave thee so many Talents. What hast thou done with them?" ' There is the Wade letter, in which he prays that the wretchedness of his case may be divulged to the world. But these passionate utterances of self-accusation begin to alternate with much more pertinent, and for Coleridge much more valuable self-inquiry—occasional humorous-regretful interest in the strange character, in 'S.T.C.,' so much in the foreground at this time. Laughter, even, at the resolutions of this man always resolving to resolve.

Another sign of revival is the returning self-respect which returning activities began to give him—not the *Friend*, because of its wretched failure, nor the early lectures, because in spite of their fashionable success they must have been connected in his mind with chances ruinously thrown away. Not even *Biographia*, because its sale was so slow, its publication so muddled,

---

[1] *U.L.*, i. 432.   [2] 651 f.

and the *Edinburgh Review* so crushing. But *Remorse* must have been more popular than he expected, and there were the later lecture courses, and, above all, the young men who from them came to acknowledge Coleridge as their leader. Coleridge began gradually to regain his lost nerve for life. *Biographia Literaria* is a half-way mark in the rehabilitation. It has the tentative confidence of an exculpation; Coleridge awkwardly tries to unsay former humilities—tries specifically to qualify the self-subjugation of the lines *To William Wordsworth* with this corollary: 'By what I *have* effected am I to be judged by my fellow-men; what I *could* have done is a question for my own conscience. . . .'

Finally, now that he was released from Wordsworth, there were new relationships to support him. The Morgans, the Gillmans, the Aderses, Frere—all friendships originating in an affectionate and admiring sympathy. And, later still, there were to be disciples —Allsop, J. H. Green.

These are some of the landmarks of Coleridge's return. It was slow and discontinuous, the friendships which helped it were all more dependent on the comfort of admiration. Coleridge, till the end of his life, was a convalescent. He was never able to overcome the loss of the opportunity which unhappiness had offered him of changing the direction of his life —the 'wasted talents' cry comes from a half-consciousness of this. Up to the end, there is the shadow of a life cut short, pathetically represented by a partial and now only petty subservience to the self-avoiding drug which he made the symbol of his downfall. Right up to the end (as late, at any rate, as 1832) he prophesies 'final emancipations' from the 'fearful slavery'[1]—all followed by secret letters to Mr. Dunn, the chemist at Highgate.

But 'Coleridge' was not dead. If he ceased to progress, he was not static. The lesson of his tragedy was always before him: that acknowledged wishes and hidden needs must be *one*: consciousness must be taken deeper still, so that the gap may be bridged to the point of coincidence. The rest of Coleridge's life and work are a pushing downward and downward in an effort to know, in order once more to be.

There is a well-known change of one kind, an outward difference. The centre of Coleridge's activity swings steadily from philosophy to religion. Not only is it the more general preoccupation of his letters, but (after *Biographia*) of his writings: the titles of his books, their subject-matter, the final paragraphs, with their capital letters, are all rounded off with religion. Yet in spite of appearances, Coleridge's purpose with religion and philosophy is the same—the pursuit of consciousness below consciousness. I recalled how, before Coleridge was submerged, he tried to make the experience from nature more fully part of himself by knowing it, evolving a philosophy of the imagination which included but was larger than that experience. Now, Coleridge wanted to relate his philosophy of the imagination with a religion which in turn included but was larger than that philosophy; in which he was

_____
[1] *L.*, 760.

to find the root from which all the faculties existent and potential in man spring. In the *Biographia* he is coining a new word, 'esemplastic,' in place of the now inadequate 'imagination.' Long inadequate, for the 'Reason and Understanding' distinction he had begun to use already as early as 1806, in an attempt to trace his earlier 'imagination and fancy' distinction nearer to its roots of divergence. What he says of 'reason'[1] is to be all the time connected with this daring descent into knowledge hitherto unspoken: because Reason is 'the *same* faculty which, as intuitive, grasps the highest truths, and which, as speculative, develops them philosophically.'

A superb adventure—but not the usual picture of Coleridge's later life, which, in some of its aspects, was not so admirable—is not always regarded as being superb at all. Coleridge's concentration on religion is more generally thought of as a rush for safety, the hurried erection of a spiritual parasol, protective against the burning criticisms of disillusioned friends, Edinburgh reviewers, and God. Why such uncharitable errors?

Recollect that the carcase washed up on the shores of England in 1806 was stripped of all but the framework of a man, and that this framework, this ego, this dead habitual shape was S.T.C., insupportably humiliated, longing for narcotic, or spiritual, props. Just because S.T.C. was never transcended—because in some respects the character, as Coleridge aged, became, as characters do, more dominant, the dependence on

[1] *U.L.*, i. 359.

props, so far from being outgrown, became more urgent. Coleridge himself fosters the confusion. In 1814, for instance, he says in one of the many synopses of his *magnum opus* that its object is 'a philosophical defence of the Articles of the Church, as far as they represent doctrine, as points of faith.'[1] This is certainly the wrong way to put it, and belongs to a desire in Coleridge which was only 'elm, not oak' rooted in himself, to *make* philosophy lead up to religion. Harmonising with this can be cited Coleridge's anxiety, soon after his return from Malta, to explain the Trinitarianism which had replaced his Unitarianism in terms of philosophy;[2] the too great eagerness to turn against the 'gross materialism' of Schelling[3]—turning against a former self in this apostasy. He tends to apply the criterion of the extent, even the extent of the devoutness, of their preoccupation with God as a standard of validity for all philosophers ('the inevitable result of all consequent reasoning in which the intellect refuses to acknowledge a higher or deeper ground than it can itself supply—and seems to possess within itself the centre of its own system—is Pantheism').

The answer to the paradox is, I believe, in the title to this book. Is that when Coleridge speaks of 'God as the only solution—God the one before all and of all, and through all,'[4] or when he says that he is trying to make all his thoughts and activities lead to the knowledge of God, and talks of religion as 'the flower and crowning blossom of the plant,'[5] it is the voice of two

---

[1] 659.   [2] *B.L.*, i. xlvii.   [3] *B.L.*, i. lxxii.
[4] *B.L.*, i. lxxiv.   [5] J.H.M., 217.

distinct men using the same words for their divergent, for entirely unrelated, thoughts. Part of Coleridge, the character on which in his weakness he had to fall back so often in these later years, needed protection, needed a religion which promised future life, a concrete paradise, and a white-out-of-black redemption from sin. He could not, wounded as he was, stand alone. But at the same time, in his true self, religion to him had reference to an act of consciousness, by which he submerged his own will with the Will of Life, an act of creation, of abandonment to the stream of life, in the manner which had been so strikingly natural to Coleridge in his less articulate, but less impeded, youth. So under the same misleading name, 'religion,' the true and the superficial Coleridge, Coleridge and S.T.C., with fundamentally dissimilar purpose, find themselves verbally active for the same thing.

In spite of the cross-purposes, Coleridge achieved in these last years some of his greatest acts of consciousness. What he says of God from this enlarged knowledge is more profound than any of his former sayings. His words have the strict 'Coleridge' quality; the same differential which is in his earliest writings. So that the words of the *Religious Musings*

> There is one Mind, one omnipresent Mind,
> Omnific. His most holy name is Love.
> Truth of subliming import! with the which
> Who feeds and saturates his constant soul,
> He from his small particular orbit flies
> With blest outstarting!

are from the same stem as his words on the 'fullest sense of faith,' written more than thirty years later,[1] when he describes faith as the 'obedience of the individual to reason,' meaning by 'reason' the faculty by which the universal Will is apprehended.

Coleridge was a very old man, physically, when he reached sixty: but there are delightful youth reminders. Very funny letters occasionally, not at all old man's jocosity. His reputation was beginning to rise high —esoterically, it was very, very high. He made a surprise journey to Cambridge two years before his death, and was received with a strange kind of enthusiasm. At Highgate he was becoming a kind of landmark, to be treated with half-amused respect. His public character, too, was altering. He was no longer regretted as a man who had committed some kind of suicide; much less, now, was he 'wife-deserter,' or ratted Jacobin. The enthusiasm of the young men, impossible as his contemporaries found it not to smile (Charles Lamb cannot help laughing at the thought of Edward Irving, a religious leader himself, writing a dedication, disciple-wise, to dear S.T.C.), was beginning to tell. The public began to expect to see in him the outward signs of elderly sapience. It seemed right that he should become, *faute de mieux*, a patriarch. A new brand of story began to be circulated about him. He is a kindly eccentric. The Highgate children (whom he calls Kingdom of Heaven-ites) are terrified of his 'Cyclopean figure and learned language.' He waylays the baker's boy to tell him 'that he never knew a

[1] *L.R.*, iv.

man good because he was religious, but that he has known one religious because he was good,"[1] and so on. In his letters it is really true that there is a new quality which neither the public nor those who listened to the Thursday evening monologues ever knew—an understanding geniality. It almost seems as if at the end of his life he began to make the kind of acceptance which leads to serenity. He accepts the sadness of age —as in *Work without Hope*:

> All Nature seems at work . . .
> And I the while, the sole unbusy thing,
> Nor honey make, nor pair, nor build, nor sing.

He accepts the fact of physical decay and alteration rather humorously, making fun of what Keats described as his alderman-after-dinner pace when he tries to walk up Highgate Hill. Or rather sadly and incredulously:

> I see those locks in silvery slips,
> This drooping gait, this altered size . . .

But

> Life is but thought: so think I will
> That Youth and I are house-mates still.

Sometimes—very rarely—there is a poem which has more than a hint of old fascinating metrical irresponsibilities; the spontaneous:

> Flowers are lovely; Love is flower-like;
> Friendship is a sheltering tree;
> O! the joys that came down shower-like,
> Of Friendship, Love, and Liberty,
>   Ere I was old!

[1] A.G.L., 144.

He tries to accept, even, the fact of once-fruitful relationships, friendships which helped to bring tremendous new Coleridges into being, now dwindled to old acquaintance. 'Old Friends burn dim. . . . Love them for what they are; nor love them less, Because to thee they are not what they were.'

Coleridge was still alive. Of the philosophy he had set out in the *Biographia Literaria* he says, within a month of his death, 'it is unformed and immature; it contains the fragments of the truth, but it is not fully thought out.' The thinking out, the reduction to complete consciousness, had been the work of the intervening twenty years: 'It is wonderful to myself to think how infinitely more profound my views now are, and yet how much clearer they are withal. The circle is completing; the idea is coming round to and to be the common sense.'[1] He has meditated so often on those truths, that they have become part of his feelings—part of himself.

I begin now to look round for a Coleridge quotation suitable as a signature to this chapter. I think—of a bibliographical detail. Preface to *Christabel*. In 1816 Coleridge wrote: 'Since the latter date (1800) my poetic powers have been, till very lately, in a state of suspended animation. . . . I trust that I shall be able to embody in verse the three parts yet to come, in the course of the present year.' This, with its hopeful 'till very lately,' was repeated in every edition up till 1829. Not omitted by him till 1834.

Or it would be suitable—it is perhaps very important

[1] J.H.M.

—to point out that when Coleridge was really dying, all the valetudinarianism, lack of stoicism, desperate cries for help, resorting to wild remedies, gave place to dignity. The letter to Green: He notices on his face the 'peculiar red streak' . . . of *Erisypelatoid Erythema*.

> Now as I should like to see you before I went, if to go I am, and leave with you the sole Depositorium of my mind and aspirations, which God may suggest to me—therefore if you can, come to me during the week. (712)

His death had a calmness in 1834 that it certainly would not have had twenty-five years earlier.

Or I think a good metaphor for the end of Coleridge's life would be this note—if we think of Coleridge as a conduit too delicate for the impulsive stream of life which rushed through him, leaving him at last fragile, worn out, bemused, with only a few drops of its essence left as token:

> If a man could pass through Paradise in a dream, and have a flower presented to him as a pledge that his soul had really been there, and if he found that flower in his hand when he awoke—Aye! and what then? (189)

Epitaphs.
> They and they only can acquire the philosophic imagination, the sacred power of self-intuition, who within themselves can interpret and understand the symbol, that the wings of the air-sylph are forming within the skin of the caterpillar; those only, who

feel in their own spirits the same instinct, which impels the chrysalis of the horned fly to leave room in its involucrum for antennae yet to come. They know and feel, that the *potential* works *in* them, even as the *actual* works on them.

*

To carry on the feelings of childhood into the powers of manhood; to combine the child's sense of wonder and novelty with the appearances, which every day for perhaps forty years had rendered familiar . . . this is the character and privilege of genius.

3

S.T.C.

. . . his faults are not positive vices, but spring entirely from defect of character.—*Coleridge on Richard II.*

'COLERIDGE,' the Coleridge of constant change and unpredictable action, is not the familiar Coleridge. I suppose it is natural that the Coleridge of this chapter, this stage 'S.T.C.', should be better known. Even among his contemporaries, though it is true that for those who knew him personally and sympathetically 'Coleridge' outshone the mannerism of character which was the mundane setting to his spirit, yet for the rest, for those who knew him only through his published, and therefore through his more estecean work, 'S.T.C.' must have seemed the only man there. No one can deny his ubiquity. In his MS. corrections, his prefaces, his method of publishing, his walk, his way of taking snuff, his lesser poems, his marriage, his capital letters, his advice to his son, his tendency to lecture, 'S.T.C.' is the obvious thing, early in his life, and late. As Coleridge himself says, 'before I was eight years old I was a *character*.'[1] Traits which were to become permanent 'were even then prominent and manifest.' And for this reason, that the character is famous, ubiquitous, and unflagging, it is worth setting out

[1] 529,

again in full incredible detail, so that the Coleridge
reader may more easily recognise the chaff from the
grain, so that he may say: 'Yes—I know, this is only
the mannerism of Coleridge's personality; he is here
lapsing into his habits of character: with respectful
sympathy I will skip this.' Only the readers who do
not understand Coleridge's greatness will linger to in-
dulge in Homeric laughter.

Here follow the traits of S.T.C.

Most obvious and permeating is a horror of 'ought.'
An inability to act from a sense of duty.

'Tremendous as a Mexican god is a strong sense of
duty.'

The trait appeared very early, first as a habit of
laziness. In '94 he refers to it, in his grand Schiller tone
of the time, as a weakness of genius: 'There is a vice
of such powerful venom, that one grain of it will
poison the overflowing goblet of a thousand virtues.
This vice constitution seems to have implanted in me,
and habit has made it almost Omnipotent. It is
indolence!' In the same letter are lines of poetry
in which he refers to the possession of great talents
which are 'sloth-jaundiced.'[1] In '96 he is suggesting a
cause—the cause—inability to work to order. . . . 'I
have received my pay beforehand . . .'[2] 'Oh, way-
ward and desultory spirit of genius! Ill canst thou
brook a taskmaster!' All this is still written with a
youthful enjoyment in and dramatisation of these
flaws. But by 1799 he is beginning to be seriously

[1] *L.*, 105.   [2] 559.

oppressed by the demands of honour, the desire to show something in return for the Wedgwood annuity, the granting of which seems to have imposed a kind of impotence on him. 'Till I have done my life of Lessing,' he says, 'till I have given the Wedgwoods some proof that I am *endeavouring* to do well for my fellow-creatures, I cannot stir.'[1] In 1803 he is groaning over 'these burrs by day of the will and the reason, these total eclipses by night!'[2] Bad health, he says, has increased his helplessness in face of the 'ought.' In 1814 he confesses how this aspect of his character was exaggerated by the effects of drugs: 'The worst was, that in *exact proportion* to the *importance* and *urgency* of any Duty was it, as of a fatal necessity, sure to be neglected:'[3] Mark that any weakness which threw Coleridge back on himself, *i.e.*, back on his character, threw S.T.C. into prominence. Late in his life, he writes to Green, at large, of the misery of that condition in which the impulse waxes as the motive wanes, saying that there should be a *Maison de Santé* for lunacy and idiocy of the *will*. 'Had such a house of health been in existence, I know who would have entered himself as a patient some five and twenty years ago.'[4] This was written in 1833.

With this 'ought' phobia goes its reverse. Coleridge was at his best when nothing was expected of him. In no author is the difference between public and private writing more marked. His best lectures, all agree, were unprepared, or off the proposed subjects. His best prose is often to be found written down the

[1] *L.*, 321.   [2] *L.*, 441.   [3] 653.   [4] *L.*, 768.

margins of a borrowed book, with no care taken about its preservation; and of these notes themselves it happens as often as not that the most valuable matter is to be found in a parenthesis.

Coleridge's own theory of the matter is interesting because it fits so closely with modern psychological dogma. 'I had begun a task and found it pleasant,' he records in a note.

> Why did I neglect it? Because I ought not to have done this. The same applies to the reading and writing of letters, essays, etc. Surely this is well worth a serious analysis, that, by understanding, I may attempt to heal it. For it is a deep and wide disease in my moral nature, at once elm-and-oak-rooted. Is it love of liberty, of spontaneity or what? These all express, but do not explain the fact. (165)

This will not do. The pioneer of psychology tries to be more precise:

> After I had got into bed last night I said to myself that I had been pompously enunciating as a difficulty, a problem of easy and common solution—viz., that it was the effect of association. From infancy up to manhood, under parents, schoolmasters, inspectors, etc., our pleasures and pleasant self-chosen pursuits (self-chosen because pleasant, and not originally pleasant because self-chosen) have been forcibly interrupted, and dull unintelligible rudiments, or painful tasks imposed upon us instead. Now all duty is felt as a command, and every command must offend. (166)

Coleridge has got to what would now be considered a 'correct' explanation of the theory, though on waking up next morning it seems to him all nonsense. Proof that it is nonsense—'he has observed the same phenomenon (of revolt against a command) in Hartley when he was only two or three months old.' We know how little a modern psychologist would consider this a disproof. Coleridge, mistrusting his own intuition, has gone back to an older explanation of the phenomenon, learnt from the philosopher after whom his son was named.

A further note, connected with this strange trait. If things were easy for Coleridge, he became inert. The Wedgwood annuity was the most unfortunate circumstance of his life. Conversely, if things were difficult, he excelled. His talk was best in the company of his most formidable rivals. In semi-consciousness of this fascinating insanity he tried to arrange adverse conditions for himself—*e.g.* for his paper the *Friend*, obtaining his paper from A, writing it hundreds of miles away at B, taking the copy to be printed sixteen miles away over a high mountain at C, and having it sold at D. This must be the explanation of his symbolically eccentric walk, as observed in earlier life by Hazlitt—walking in uneasy diagonals, from one side of the road to the other; a habit noticed again much later by Carlyle, who wrongly diagnosed the crisscross perambulation of the back garden at Highgate as a mark of indecision. Coleridge himself told Hazlitt that he 'liked to compose in walking over uneven ground, or breaking through the straggling branches of a copse-wood.' Compare the first version of *Love*, which has this stanza—afterwards omitted:

And how he crossed the Woodman's paths
  Tho' briars and swampy mosses beat,
How boughs rebounding scourged his limbs,
  And low stubs gored his feet.

How was Carlyle to know that Coleridge was turning the level paths of No. 3 the Grove into a rocky and perilous mountain track whose difficulties he was able to congratulate himself on miraculously overcoming? And compare—but the cross-references are endless. It is certain that a rub of some sort, a quarrel even, was the best way of stimulating Coleridge into some kind of action. Crabb Robinson may have been wrong in suggesting that the anti-Wordsworth passages of *Biographia* were inspired by personal bitterness, but it is possible that without that quarrel the book would never have been written.

A second characteristic. It would appear from the way in which Coleridge's 'ought' failure has been illustrated by his own self-description that consciousness of this flaw in himself must have cancelled most of its bad effects. But this consciousness only belongs to 'Coleridge'; 'S.T.C.' was far from admitting 'S.T.C.' On the contrary, 'S.T.C.' constructed a self-deceiving picture, an elaborately modelled ideal of himself, sometimes opposed, sometimes parallel, to the reality—a picture which he was always trying to justify.

The salient points of the portrait come easily to

mind—a man mild and noble, to whom the words of his own 'S.T.C.' epitaph are sympathetic. ('O lift one thought in prayer for S.T.C.') Noble, thoughtful, loving, misunderstood: unrecognised, follower of philosophy, pensive, with quiet tears upon his cheek. The Christian, the penitent, the good man. The wronged man, the loving man, the man bowed down by, but still struggling against, insupportable misfortunes. The great and good man subject to newspaper vendettas: the man of pregnant advice, which no one will take.

As a young man, especially, he assumes nobility. He repeats more than once such a phrase as 'He cannot be long wretched who dares be actively virtuous.'[1] He takes the same noble tone with Southey: Tell your aunt of Pantisocracy, he advises, but tell her 'with all possible gentleness. She has loved you tenderly; be firm, therefore, as a rock, mild as the lamb.'[2] And Coleridge even gives a noble motive for the prime weakness of S.T.C.—inability to conform with duties. 'I could not love the man who advised me to keep a school, or write for a newspaper. He must have a hard heart.'[3]

He makes determinations to live up to this picture. 'I will express *all* my feelings,' he says, 'but I will previously take care to make my feelings benevolent.' Love is part of the scheme, rectitude as well—especially at periods of moral degradation. Then he will criticise regretfully the opium drinking of Burnet, or

[1] *L.*, 125. [2] *L.*, 93.
[3] Not spoken humorously? *L.*, 190.

the excessive pipe-smoking of Charles Lamb.[1] In 1811 he is pleased to be able to say of his difficulties that it is 'Some consolation—nay, a great consolation—that they have not fallen on me thro' any vice, any extravagance or self-indulgence; but only from having imprudently hoped too highly of men. . . .'[2]

This extraordinary exaggeration of—quite unconscious—deceit is due partly to a fear of moral disapproval. If Southey is too much i' the frown (a natural revenge for Coleridge's high-horse attitude over Pantisocracy) Coleridge explains to him that the reason 'I do not enjoy your society so much, as I anticipated that I should do, is wholly or almost wholly owing to the nature of my domestic feelings, and the fear or the consciousness that you did not and could not sympathize with them.'[3] Coleridge always seemed to have some stern moral mentor in the background. It is not his father apparently who can be held responsible for this so much as the rectitude of George. 'My brother George possessed the cheering consolation of conscience, but—I am talking I know not what—yet there is a pleasure, doubtless an exquisite pleasure, mingled up in the most painful of our virtuous emotions.'[4]

'Coleridge' knew well enough that to live up to principles which were not grounded in his experience was the only sin: that brothers whose lives were firm in George's kind of faith and good conscience were unimportant. 'S.T.C.' on the contrary had a strong sense of guilt, which meant a strong sense of conven-

[1] 633.   [2] 635.   [3] 594.   [4] L., 59.

tional morality, and an unreasoning reverence for such 'upright' men.

*

Much of Coleridge's writing is full of this irrelevant morality, inexplicable until the duality is realised. One of the worst results is a puritanism which is connected with nothing and seems to fall from nowhere, soiling much of his criticism and seeming as out of place as a voice from another world. Once in his life he permitted himself to be a little free before the public—when he headed No. II of the *Watchman* as follows:

ESSAY ON FASTS

Wherefore my Bowels shall sound like an Harp.

Isaiah xvi, 11.

Subscribers objected,[1] and Coleridge never forgot the reproof; he was to make up for it later.

There are, for instance, the famous 'bitch' variants to *Christabel*.

> (Sir Leoline the baron rich
> Hath a toothless mastiff bitch.)

In response to the wishes of an 'honoured friend,' 'bitch' is changed to 'which.' Alternatively, the rhyming words are 'bold' and 'old.' Charles Lamb suggested 'round' and 'hound.' This is the standard example. The attitude is less amusing and more regrettable when it affects his criticism. With the date of Coleridge's birth in mind, the language of

[1] 559.

his puritanical objections to the eighteenth century and its 'profanation of the word Love . . . *rouged* like a harlot, and with a harlot's wanton leer,'[1] is understandable. But the irrelevance and blindness of this standard applied to Goethe is gross: 'I need not tell you that I never put pen to paper as a translator of 'Faust' . . . much of which I thought vulgar, licentious, and blasphemous.'[2] It is equally absurd when he praises Shakespeare for his lack of coarseness,[3] or details the extraordinary subtlety of Shakespeare's portrait of Edmund in *Lear* as a man suffering from the 'wormwood, Gall, Corrosive virus' etc. of the brand of bastardy.[4]

That S.T.C. and not Coleridge is talking here can be seen from the estecean phraseology of such passages —his 'horror and disgust' when he saw (as opposed to when he read) the *Beggar's Opera*.[5] 'Every innocent female must blush with shame,' etc. And *cf.* a letter of 1802 to the daughter of 'Perdita':

I have a wife, I have sons, I have an infant Daughter—what excuse could I offer to my conscience if by suffering my own name to be connected with those of Mr. Lewis, or Mr. Moore, I was the *occasion* of their reading the 'Monk,' or the wanton poems of Thomas Little Esqre? Should I not be an infamous Pander to the Devil in the Seduction of my own offspring? My head turns giddy, my heart sickens, at the very thought of seeing such books in the hands of a child of mine. (*U.L.*, i. 232)

[1] 453.   [2] 506.   [3] 337.
[4] 390.   [5] 195.

Never in his private notes does Coleridge allow this parson voice to be heard.

*

Irrelevant morality—and irrelevant ambition. Sense of guilt and that sense of wasted talents which ruinously made him redouble his efforts to live up to the unreal, ideal self of S.T.C.'s picture—all this, combined with his natural thirst of spirit to have something honourable to say of himself, led to those long lists of projected works that never came off, to 'spawning plans like a herring,' as Southey said, plans which were many of them contrary to the true direction of 'Coleridge.'

The first Scheme to be formed—and therefore, of course, not to mature—was the Book of Pantisocracy. A typical example, because the pamphlet of pantisocracy would in any case have been the least important thing about it. There is much of the true Coleridge in the formulation of these projects. What Browning wanted comfortingly to say to Waring, he could truly have said to Coleridge—that merely to have thought of such projects was genius; because the new direction, the new attitude to life and the knowledge which gave birth to them was so truly original. The outline of the *magnum opus*, the abstract of the epic poem, the idea of writing a *Recluse*, a *Faust*, or Hymns to the Elements is true Coleridge. What is estecean is the serious undertaking, widely advertised, of hopelessly colossal tasks (as if 'bigness were greatness') such as the suggestion in *Letters*, 425, which made Southey smile so sadly, that between them they should produce a 'Bibliotheca

Britannica, or an History of British Literature, bibliographical, and critical. The two *last* volumes I would
have to be a chronological catalogue of all noticeable
or extant books. . . . I will, with great pleasure, join
you in learning Welsh and Erse. . . . If the Spanish
neutrality continues, I will go in October or November
to Biscay, and throw light on the Basque. . . . Then
let the fourth volume take up the history of metaphysics, theology, medicine, alchemy, common canon,
and Roman law, from Alfred to Henry vii. . . .'[1]
The mere sketching in of the separate mountain ranges
of these tasks seems to convince him that he is already
hard at work for humanity. He appears in these
curious sentences to be talking to himself, attempting
to bewitch himself, in the dreaming voice with which
he once said to Southey:

'I have very serious Thoughts of trying to get a
couple of Pupils, very serious ones.' (*U.L.*, i. 129)

It is part self-deception, part desire to rehabilitate
himself in the eyes of the world, and part a trick to
force some sort of action out of himself. He seems to
be thinking: 'If I seriously let *this* honourable friend
know that I am well forward with this plan, then
nothing can prevent my doing it—I am lost if I don't.'
This may account for the direct lies he tells, to George
Coleridge, *e.g.* in 1809:

a large volume of Poems, another of political
Memoirs and statistic papers on Naples, Malta,

[1] *L.*, 427.

Sicily, Oegypt, and the Coast of Africa, my Greek and Latin accidence, vocabulary of Fernsmaker and G. and L. philosoph. Grammar and Introduction to Logic, with the History of Logic, from Zeno to the French Pseudo-Logician Condillac *etc.*, which are ready for the Press as soon as I can procure the Paper, (*U.L.*, ii. 13)

all practically non-existent. And again, to his old friend, Daniel Stuart, telling him (in 1814) that a *magnum opus* is printing at Bristol—even telling Dorothy Wordsworth that he has finished his number of the *Friend* when she knows, and he knows she knows, that not a line has been written.

*

Self-deception sets up a vicious circle. If it is un-acknowledged, fresh deceptions have to be resorted to in order to counteract the feelings of inferiority and worthlessness which are its unconscious result. I am plunging into our contemporary psychology. Perhaps I am putting the cart before the horse. Perhaps I am too much affected by current terms when I want to lay a further group of characteristics under the heading, Sense of Inferiority. I will set these out, leaving all psychological conclusions unconcluded, demonstrating them myself merely, as the curious detail of the false Coleridge.

Whether or not, then, it comes from some irrational sense of inferiority (likely to be emphasised by contrast with the well-grounded and successful characters of intimates like Southey and Wordsworth) there is Coleridge's tendency to preach—'my old vice of preaching,'[1] as he calls it. It is most clearly shown in a kind of desire to establish a psychological advantage over the audience, single or multiple, whom he is addressing. It is often apparent in letters. The tendency is strong in youth, and strong again at a later period, when in the world's eye he possesses less right to the habit than most. He is sometimes obviously convincing himself that he has the right to preach, as when in 1803 he talks with pity of the 'helplessly self-tormented Burnet'[2]—a drug taker. The attitude is muddled by a desire to be liked, and complicated by his real superiority, plus a natural desire that it should be recognised, plus a desire to demonstrate that it ought to be recognised, plus a wish for the kind of reverence only granted to the unconsciously superior.

A ludicrous aspect of this preaching voice, which makes isolated and startling appearances in letters, is that it is often the voice of Pecksniff. He can say things which are perfectly true, even profound, and destroy them by Pecksniffian phraseology. 'Surely, said I, I have trifled with the spirit of love, and it has passed away from me!'[3] True, this is from an early letter. It is partly the language of his age. Take a letter from 1824. Coleridge makes a profound remark on Volition —and then turns it into farce by adding: 'My dear Sir, am I under the inebriation of Self-conceit? I trust not.'[4] Or he will suddenly, half-way through an otherwise sane letter, throw himself back in his chair, as it were, look at the ceiling, and remark: 'What are

[1] *U.L.*, i. 104.   [2] *U.L.*, i. 240.   [3] *L.*, 103.   [4] *U.L.*, ii. 335.

our Lives? Accidents.'[1] He follows the very technique of Pecksniff bathos when he rounds off his rectitude capital-letter-wise only to give himself away, momentarily but completely, in the last sentence:

> My health is in a most distressful state; my Bowel and Stomach attacks frequent and alarming. But I bear Pain with a woman's Fortitude; it is constitutional with me to look quietly and steadily in its face, as it were, and to ask it—What and Whence it is?
> If this Letter reach you in time, you will oblige me by going to the best Druggist in Kendal for me, and purchasing an ounce of crude opium, and 9 ounces of Laudanum, the latter put in a stout bottle. (*U.L.*, i. 297)

Like Pecksniff, too, he seems unattractively incapable of regarding his vices with any kind of Falstaffian light-heartedness. He has been to a New Year's party. He has to refuse an invitation for the following day in consequence. He had been desired, he explains, to drink one glass in honour of the departing year. 'Though the glasses were very small, yet such was the effect produced during my sleep, that I awoke unwell, and in about twenty minutes after had a relapse of my bilious complaint.'[2]

And add to this—though it is less Pecksniff than Micawber—Coleridge's tendency to make a meal out of a crisis, to come out strong in a situation. The standard instance of this must be the letters he wrote

---

[1] *U.L.*, ii. 27.   [2] *B.E.*, i. 52.

to Lamb after Lamb's great tragedy.[1] But merely to be made a godfather seemed to draw from Coleridge a curious insincerity of phraseology. . . . 'I shall be much gratified by standing beside the baptismal font as one of the sponsors of the little pilgrim at his inauguration into the rights and duties of Immortality.' And there is the same kind of unfeeling feeling when he comments on real tragedy, on his friend Tom Wedgwood, slowly dying of a painful disease.

'A man of genius . . . exquisite taste . . . noble Father . . . large Fortune, a fine person, a most benevolent Heart . . .

— and what more can you think as constituent of compleat Happiness! All these thing unite in T. Wedgwood: and all these things are blasted by —a thickening of the Gut! O God! Such a Tree, in full blossom—it's fruits all medicinal and foodful— and a grub—a grub at the root! (*U.L.*, i. 247)

Coleridge does not seem to be really perceptive of sorrow except in himself—and even in himself it was a slow and laborious process. A Coleridge is too heterogeneous a unit to write well, or with true apprehension, of sorrow in others. He tells the story of how, after parting with Keats at the end of their famous hour's walk at Highgate, he remarked: 'There is death in that hand!' It comes as a faint shock only to learn that he made this prophecy of other people, perhaps several other people, besides Keats. It is impossible not to suspect that, in the case of Keats, he was lucky.

[1] *Cf. post*, p. 164.

What chiefly harmed Coleridge in the eyes of his friends was that this preaching, prophetic tone usually took the form of criticism, as in the tremendous sermonising letter to Southey, a reproach for the break up of Pantisocracy. Again, his motive seems to have been anxiety to avoid the criticism of others.

Very often in his life Coleridge was morbidly sensitive to criticism. How many hours did he not spend thinking of the tittle-tattle of the *Anti-Jacobin*, forgotten by everybody else, describing him as having 'commenced citizen of the world, left his poor children fatherless, and his wife destitute.' The *Biographia*, classic example of the mixed estecean and Coleridgean, is constantly lapsing into long exculpatory footnotes (made footnotes to emphasise their importance) complaining of the 'unfair attacks' of the *Edinborough* and Hazlitt. The attacks were unfair indeed, but Coleridge's character was ill vindicated by the violence of S.T.C.'s denials. This amounts at certain periods of his life almost to persecution mania. *Cf.* the letter of 1807,[1] where he is so disproportionately angry with Sheridan for making very good fun of a very bad line in *Osorio*, and denies ever having written the line in question. Or the letter of 1816, where he so violently exculpates himself from Crabb Robinson's suggestion that he does not always return borrowed books:

Yesterday I had an opportunity of cross-questioning him. Robinson, I have borrowed more books from you than from all my acquaintance collec-

[1] *U.L.*, i. 376.

tively. . . . Have I ever lost one? No.—Have I ever retained your books beyond the given time without obtaining your permission? No.—Then you ought in justice to do your best to contradict the calumny, which your knowledge of poor Charles Lamb's Character ought to have prevented you from helping to spread. (*U.L.*, ii. 173)

'Mania' is the wrong word. What drives Coleridge almost to madness is the right intuition that his faults are *not his fault*, that they come from poor Coleridge's character, from this unescapable old man of the sea, which has nothing to do with 'Coleridge.' 'Cruelly, I well know, have I been calumniated,' he says in the sad letter to Wedgwood on the occasion of the withdrawal of his annuity, 'and even my faults (the sinking under the sense of which has been itself one of the greatest) have been attributed to dispositions absolutely opposite to the real ones—and—and . . .' Coleridge himself was beyond criticism. All the more temptation to aim shafts at the easy mark of S.T.C. The attackers could be so confidently in the right. In his later and calmer life Coleridge was inclined to agree with the rumour that the Reviews had something to do with the death of Keats.

Almost as strong as his fear of criticism was his desire for love and encouragement. Here the two sides of Coleridge merge confusingly. He was capable of making productive contacts—was able to evolve through such relationships . . . and then (quite irrelevantly) his weaker side needed support of some uncritical, praising kind, no matter whence it came. 'To be beloved is all I need,'[1] he says, and confesses to a 'cowardly dread of being hated even by bad men.'[2] He is proud of praise even if it does not come from very discriminating people; is unreservedly devoted to the giver of unreserved praise; likes to record successes with men of importance—even if the importance is worldly only: 'Lord Darnley, who was always very courteous to me, took this with a pleasant nod of his head.'[3] The worst aspect of this trait was the sudden and intense conviction he would assume that some much-loved friend was slighting him. The letters to Poole at the end of 1795, written because he imagines that for some reason Poole is unwilling to have him as a neighbour at Stowey, show how he could work on himself. 'The Damp struck into my very heart; and there I feel it. . . .'

> Mrs. Coleridge has observed the workings of my face while I have been writing, and is entreating to know what is the matter. I dread to show her your letter. I dread it. My God! my God! What if she should dare to think that my most beloved friend has grown cold towards me! . . . (569)

This exaggerated sensibility, joined with a deficiency in worldly good sense, or tact, led to a hampering lack of homogeneity in all Coleridge's worldly actions and the conduct of his affairs. He could never be 'right' in everyday matters. The worst drawback of this was that it endangered those friendships which he

[1] 115. [2] 608. [3] 483.

was capable of exchanging so fully.[1] 'I detest profession,'[2] he says—but is often professing. In spite of Southey's remonstrance against this very habit[3] he continues to distress him with emotional adulation.

His friends must have disliked, also, the manner of extreme self-abasement which he sometimes adopted. He had no quickness of sensibility in the superficialities of human contact, nor had he the kind of good sense and social experience which makes a man able to be contained, to gain effects through economy, and so forth. On his correspondents, especially, he often made a confused impression of insincerity. One reason for this was that he frequently made the mistake of writing what he thought would please; going so far, sometimes, as to affect the manner of his correspondents. Writing to Southey he is particularly full of hard-work talk and introduces an occasional 'Southeianism' as he called it, *i.e.* a rather broad kind of jocularity.[4] He reflects Poole's tone in his letters to Poole. To his brother George he writes dependably[5]—for fourteen years I have been 'never in debt,' and so on. It is all a question of worldly tact. A question of knowing that though he might have powers of real sincerity above any in his generation, though he might have that god-like gift, yet at the same time much misunderstanding would have been saved had he known that a kind of superficial sincerity, a simple dependability, is helpful by way of introduction.

---

[1] *Cf.* pp. 156 f for a fuller discussion of this trait.
[2] *U.L.*, i. 73.   [3] *L.*, 488.
[4] *U.L.*, i. 127.   [5] *U.L.*, ii. 13, 17.

Wasted energies, again. If some worldly thing goes wrong with him, no pride in stoicism, no cutting losses. If he is insulted, or wrongfully accused, no useful firmness of dealing to fall back on, only nights of indecision followed by some tentative half measure. If some worldly thing goes right with him, it is almost as bad. If a rich friend offers some much-needed loan, he goes through all the agonies of not accepting it, followed by all the agonies of accepting it, followed by all the agonies of longing to repay it, and all the agonies of taking no steps whatever to do so. What can Byron have thought of a letter of acknowledgment which started like this:

> MY LORD,
> I have to acknowledge the receipt of your Letter with the 100£ inclosed. What can I say? Till a Friend and House-mate addressed me at my bed-side, with—'You have had a letter franked by Lord Byron? Is it from *him*?' I had, as it were, forgotten that I was myself the object of your kindness—so completely lost was I in thinking of the thing itself and the manner in which it was done.   (662)

Writing a similar letter, for a similar reason, to T. Allsop, easily young enough to be his son, he confesses: 'Why should I hesitate to tell you? I burst into a flood of tears.'
                                    *

It would be possible to take various years, various activities in Coleridge's life and demonstrate them as fields of battle in which first one side and then the other was victorious. I have tried to trace the estecean element in one strand of his life elsewhere,[1] choosing an example which displays with horrifying fullness the crippling process of waste and misplaced effort entailed—Coleridge's marriage. In his relations with his wife, 'Coleridge' is most obscured. He seems to have acted from a mood, a flurry; or from a theory; never from the spontaneous simplicity of his true feelings. S.T.C. was not the man for stoically strategic retreats, nor for cutting losses. He was 'incapable of acting with simplicity' in such situations. Dorothy Wordsworth's bitter criticism is true—with the reservation that the failure was not in any lack of depth or integrity: it was the unbalancing eddy of S.T.C., its upsetting cross-current, which made all seem unreal, which made important issues seem suddenly like shadows, so that he could neither love his wife, nor leave her, with the strength and directness of his true personality. He understood her character so well, and that the last thing it was susceptible to was advice: and yet with insane indifference to laws of psychology which he was the first to enunciate, advice was all he could give her.

S.T.C. is in evidence, then, when Coleridge is acting in any official capacity, such as Husband—when he is engaged in one of the regular and recognised functions of life. (One wishes there was more record of Coleridge at Malta, the only time when he came near to being engaged in routine work.) As a husband—or as a father. Coleridge as father would be a good subject for this thesis. There is the real Coleridge, with his

[1] S.P.

very young son, making beautifully sensitive and affectionate perceptions of his child's behaviour,[1] of the look of his tears in the moonlight, of the way he 'uses the air of the breezes as skipping ropes,' of his thought processes when he is disobedient. There is S.T.C. when Hartley is a little older, trying to make up for his earlier deficiencies in parental sternness by the concentrated advice of a letter,[2] almost a threatening letter, full of the contemporary tendency to keep children down, a tendency which had its religious foundation in a doctrine of original sin so framed that the possibility of original virtue was left out.

'Specially,' Coleridge writes, 'never pick at or snatch up anything, eatable or not . . . it is a dirty trick; and people of weak stomachs would turn sick at a dish which a young *filthpaw* had been fingering. . . . Among the lesser faults I beg you to endeavour to remember not to stand between the half-opened door. . . . But come *in* or go out . . . and, be assured, I am not writing in anger, but on the contrary with great love.'

The love is commendable considering the accusation in the postscript:

> P.S. I have not spoken about your mad passions and frantic looks and pout-mouthing; because I trust that is all over.

All over, surely, now that Hartley had reached the age of ten.

It is typical of S.T.C. that with a kind of afterthought solicitude he should begin now to care after his children,

---

[1] *Cf.* J.L.L., 454. [2] *L.*, 620.

and in the wrong way. Half consciously he is aware that some of his own characteristics are re-emerging in his children, and he starts the familiar vicious circle by prohibitory 'oughts' and psychologically clumsy 'dont's.' In the same letter he warns Hartley against 'this power which you possess of shoving aside all disagreeable reflections, or losing them in a labyrinth of day-dreams. . . .' Hartley did turn out to be very like 'a near relation of his,' as Mrs. C. said. Later in life he became almost a complete S.T.C., without the Pecksniffisms, but with only a fascinating hint of the counteracting, all-cancelling Coleridge. As his father said, deeply understanding: 'it is the absence of Self . . . that is the mortal Sickness of Hartley's Being. . . .'[1]

Coleridge's sons were fond of their father, and were proud of him. Probably Derwent knew how to smile at the incomparable esteceanism of the letters he was sent at Cambridge. Derwent had turned out, very temporarily, to be a man of Dress, and Family Visiting. Coleridge attacks Coxcombry. Coleridge contrasts *himself* at Cambridge—regular studious hours, followed by studious talk. 'With what delight did I not resume my reading in my own Rooms at Jesus each following morning. Think you a Ball or a Concert or a Lady Party, or a Literary Club, would have left me in the same state? . . . I am not angry . . . but it is calamitous that you do not know how anxiously and affectionately I am your *Father*.'

And the postscript:

[1] *U.L.*, ii. 309.

P.S.   I hear that you are Premier or Secretary of a Literary Club—about old Books—If such things did not dissipate your time or thought, they *dissipate* and perplex your *character*. They are well maybe for B.A.s and M.A.s.

Even S.T.C. should have left out the warning about old books.

It really seems as if the sad decay of Hartley—he lost his fellowship at Oriel on the grounds of intemperance—was a back-wash of the dark estecean powers. It is not suggested that this assertion is verifiable. But any survey of a Character will show how potent the fixed unadaptability of character can be—in some cases how powerful for evil. The most tragic aspect of S.T.C. lies in the fact that, as a character, it was never anything but a handicap.

There are three ways in which a character can be actually useful to the possessor. It can be worldly; it can be reverable; it can be lovable. The man of worldly character has an asset whose material fruits he can enjoy: he can fall back on the pleasures of mundane success. Coleridge's character was actually anti-worldly—something impelled him, in the face of his wish for public recognition, to ensure public coldness towards his activities. This is best exemplified by his publication methods. Most of his books were failures before they appeared, either because printing and distribution arrangements had been muddled, or because they had been delayed and delayed until all topical flavour had evaporated. *Watchman* and *Friend* are well-known examples. *Biographia* should have appeared when Wordsworth's new weird diction was still weird and new. Again, there were many reasons why it was very important for Coleridge to publish a complete edition of his poems soon after 1800. Because tentative arrangements for such a collection remained tentative, his contemporary reputation as a poet was always confused. He was connected, in a misleading way, with a 'Lake School' to which he had never belonged—which did not, in fact, exist. He delayed the publication of *Christabel* until the invention of its metre had become hackneyed through Walter Scott's imitations of it.

And consider Coleridge's choice of titles. . . . The entablatures surmounting his late pamphlets are so ponderous that it is certain their unattractiveness must permanently have affected sales. When at last Coleridge began to be accepted, and some kind of overtures were made by the big Review editors, he follows up this opening by writing a letter of suggestions to *Blackwood*, with a 'scheme on which a Magazine should be conducted.'[1]

Some characters, on the other hand, even if they are not suited to wide worldly success, can make copy out of this very deficiency, presenting to the world a *persona* of modest dependability, steadiness, or the like: they can fall back on the advantages of moral rectitude, that is. The great advantage of this gift is that it puts its possessor, so far as the world's view is concerned, in the right. But Coleridge's character never once allowed him to appear to be in the right. His particular kind of vice, and his particular kind of hypocrisy,

[1] 679.

aroused the indignation of those who consciously or unconsciously assess people from a moral point of view. S.T.C. could not get *right* with the world, could not earn respect. Too modest, or too much the great man. Puritanical, yet not pure in his own life. And most fatally, for various complex psychological reasons, he was deceitful. So that there has grown up a conventional way of writing about Coleridge which is the reverse of reverential. The tone is set by Carlyle. It is jocular, and it is pitying—almost 'poor old Coleridge.' 'Singular . . . Coleridgean moonshine.' Coleridge's vice, opium, had no picturesque-picaresque qualities. It is an unsocial habit. 'Damn you,' said John Wilson to de Quincey, when he brought his laudanum bottle with him to dinner, 'can't you take your whisky toddy like a Christian man, and leave your damned opium slops to infidel Turks, Persians, and Chinamen?' And Coleridge's way of taking opium was far less attractive than de Quincey's, because more secretive. So that ludicrous stories of the straits to which he was put to conceal his secret passed through their evolution of exaggeration. Coleridge was the sort of man, too, who got himself mixed up in mysterious and ludicrous little accidents. A cheeky parody of Sir Walter Scott, which Coleridge would have been the last person to write, appears in the *Courier* over his initials. Nor did he ever discover how it was that a man came to be found hanging in the Park wearing, for some unfathomable reason, one of S.T.C.'s shirts, so that the rumour of his suicide was spread. . . .[1]

[1] R.S., Vol. iii.

But if Coleridge was unfortunate in not having a character which could be called estimable, he was most unfortunate of all in not having a character which was widely felt as lovable or attractively clear-cut. Its inconsistency, the difficulty of placing it, seems to have been responsible. Readers and admirers were alienated by contradictions which they did not know how to take, so that what public he acquired, beyond immediate and sympathetic friends, he soon lost. To repeat his wife's words: 'I am constantly asked whether Coleridge has changed his political opinions. Pray furnish me.'

Nevertheless it is interesting that the public who insists on labelling were not beaten, even by Coleridge. Towards the end of his life they got him, giving him the quality of his seeming nebulosity, calling him vague. (Carlyle took this up, underlining it—'Kantean dream-world . . . haze-world.') But such a character is not given from personal popularity, nor out of public love, especially if with the vagueness is connected something actorish and insincere. Nor is Coleridge in his private life any more 'lovable.' He was deeply loved, by those who knew 'Coleridge'—especially by those who had known him first when he was young, whose first experience of him had been of 'Coleridge.' But 'S.T.C.' was not lovable. Coleridge knew this, and it increased the complications. He knew, for instance, that he was less popular, by public and private standards, than Wordsworth or Southey, and he probably knew the reason. 'A glow-worm with a pin stuck through it,' he quotes as a description of himself. And: 'Mine is not a *picturesque* Face; Southey's was made for a picture . . .'[1] The only inactive-introspective character ever to achieve picturesqueness was Hamlet. An early opinion on Coleridge, by an 'intelligent though matter-of-fact bystander' (Kitty Wedgwood) might have been the text for this page: 'I cannot overcome the first disagreeable impression of his accent and exterior. I confess too . . . there is in my opinion too great a parade of superior feeling; and an excessive goodness and sensibility is put forward, which gives an appearance, at least, of conceit, and excites suspicion that it is acting; as real sensibility never endeavours to excite notice. . . .'[2] Miss Wedgwood has not learnt how confusingly genius may ape pseudo-genius. Carlyle, describing Coleridge a quarter of a century later, gets nearer to the root of his unpopularity from another angle when he describes the special egotism of the character-ridden man—the only side of Coleridge which he seemed able to enlarge on, though he is aware of other Coleridges in the background. He calls him 'deficient in laughter, or indeed in sympathy for concrete human things either on the sunny or on the stormy side.' Most untrue of Coleridge; most true of S.T.C.

Most true of S.T.C.—because the character was less than a nullification—was itself a positive power. Just as the presence of Coleridge could impregnate, so the presence of S.T.C., at its thwarting and fulminating worst, could be a power of disintegration. Dorothy Wordsworth, writing to Mrs. Clarkson in one of the

[1] *U.L.,* i. 195.　　　[2] R.B.L.

hopelessly estecean middle years of Coleridge's life, warns her of this disintegrating power: 'I do sincerely wish that you may not go thither, for I know so well the power of his presence that I should dread the effects upon your health.'[1] It is a warning against the sterilising force of a Character.

Coleridge knows it all. The all-conscious man knows the contradiction in himself; and the last words on this subject should be his own.

He generalises thus on mankind from his own experience:

> one while cheerful, stirring, feeling in resistance nothing but a joy and a stimulus; another while drowsy, self-distrusting, prone to rest, loathing our own self-promises, withering our own hopes—our hopes, the vitality and cohesion of our being! (*L.*, 342)

He knows, as fully as it can be known, the difference between life and existence.

He describes the contest in himself as part of his first recollections. 'My eloquence,' he says, 'was most commonly excited by the desire of running away and hiding myself from my personal and inward feelings, *and not for the expression of them.*'[2] There is no description of the Hamlet problem more concrete than this sudden confession to Southey:

In my nature, he says, there was always

---

[1] D.S., 254.   [2] 694.

a sense of weakness, a haunting sense that I was an herbaceous plant, as large as a large tree, with a trunk of the same girth, and branches as large and shadowing, but with pith within the trunk, not heart of wood—that I had power not strength, an involuntary impostor, that I had no real Genius, no real depth. (607)

He knows the *sensation* of incompleteness which this gives him: 'I know, I feel, that I am weak, apt to faint away, inwardly self-deserted. . . .'[1] He knows the frustration of it, speaking of his character as almost 'in a moral *marasmus* from negatives.' He knows the lies and deceipts which accompany his career, he knows the false judgments to which he is liable: he realises later that the grained mannerism of age may have hardened over his spirit: 'the Snows may have drifted from my head downwards and inwards. . . .'[2]

S.T.C. sometimes seems almost to disappear in the sanction of Coleridge's knowledge—of the Coleridge who knows so well, for instance, the meaning of 'waste' or 'use' of time:

'The good man,' he wrote elsewhere, 'organizes the hours and gives them a soul, and to that, the very essence of which is to fleet and *to have been*, he communicates an imperishable and a spiritual nature. Of the good and faithful servant whose energies are thus methodized, it is less truly affirmed, that he lives in time than that time lives in him.' (J. H. M., 144)

[1] 614.   [2] 702.

If Coleridge has a true ideal—one which is valid in his own life—it is of the great in unity, of the heroes who have overcome the frustrations of character. He admires most in men the quality of homogeneity—he believes it to exist in Wordsworth, and sometimes he describes the real Coleridge best when he imagines this quality into Wordsworth—Wordsworth looking forth

> calm and sure
> From the dread watch-tower of man's absolute self.

'He is a happy man,' Coleridge writes, 'because he knows the intrinsic value of the different objects of human pursuit, and regulates his wishes in strict subordination to that knowledge.'[1] Coleridge knew that it was only in the 'homogeneous' that action bore full fruit.

*

Coleridge, in fact, knew the situation. And for that reason, he must have known, somewhere, the cause. But this knowledge of the cause was now complete, now incomplete; now above the surface, now unconscious.

S.T.C. had no doubts whatever. S.T.C. put it down, as we have seen, to the unhappy marriage—or he put it down to his health. In general, he connects the impotence of his volitional powers with bad health; in detail, he will occasionally say, in all sincerity and belief, 'strange, as it seems, the act of metre composition, as I lay in bed, perceptibly affected

[1] 612.

my inflamed eyes. . . .'[1] I believe this—but it reminded me for a moment of Mr. Rea, who in *Modern Language Notes* said that the cause of Coleridge's decay was not spiritual but was almost certainly due to 'osteomyelitis, or impacted teeth.'

Coleridge knew differently. He knew that though physical or psychological ill-health was connected with disruption of soul, it was only as a sign, not as a cause. He spent his life in trying to know the real cause, in trying to overcome the division by making it fully conscious. He explores life more and more deeply, closer and closer to the root from which all differences spring, till in his search for the cause of the contradictions in himself, his whole world seems to be made up of elements linked by contrast, and his most constant problem, the reconciliation of opposites. When his thoughts wander, the pattern forms itself . . . *the spring, with the quiet surface . . . wet soap won't stick, dry becomes sticky . . . dark with excess of light.*[2] His notebooks and his pamphlets are full of it. Observe that he early makes a division between two kinds of antithesis. First, the kind which contains a superficial dissimilarity, but a hidden relation. Such opposites, homogeneous, swinging about one axis, are Unity-and-Variety, Sameness-and-Difference.

> Rest, motion! O ye strange locks of intricate simplicity, who shall find the key? . . . Rest—enjoyment and death. Motion—enjoyment and life. O the depth of the proverb, 'Extremes meet.' (253 . . . 180)

[1] *L.*, 341.   [2] *A.P.* 19.

And then, looking into himself, Coleridge talks of the other, the true opposites, calling them contraries.[1] The connection here is superficial only, or verbal only. He pairs words to express surface, and the contrasted core; the mechanical rule, and the creating principle; the dead element and the living. Copy: imitation. Observation: meditation. Reflection: contemplation. Comprehension: apprehension. Remembrance: recollection with recognition. The agreeable: the beautiful. He is describing himself: the elements opposed in himself are behind these words.

These distinctions, reflections of 'Coleridge and S.T.C.,' of man alive and man mechanical, represent I believe the true picture; and I believe the more usual view of Coleridge, as a man who had his few years of life, and then decayed, to be false. Coleridge achieved youth: he achieved maturity also. Though he did not after the age of thirty change the direction of his life, he established its quality: this is maturity. Coleridge fell from grace. He lost integrity in the coils of the world and of his own character: but to descend to the depths is not to decay, especially if the threads of being are slowly and painfully gathered together again. In this Coleridge, not without heroism, succeeded.

The true picture, then, is not one of decay, but of eclipse. Of a true self, sometimes obscured by a monstrous, self-parodying ego. The sense of the infinite power of the word obscured by a taste for Pecksniff circumlocution: the ability to inspire obscured

[1] C.S., 24.

by the desire to preach: the capacity for real friendship obscured by characteristic dependence on sympathy: readiness for the reception of a truly moulding influence obscured by hero-worship of the comparatively unworthy: capacity for deep knowledge of men obscured by obtuseness in the superficialities of human contact: superiority to worldly cares and ambitions obscured by a maniac aversion to small but necessary duties: integrity which made it impossible for him to write down to the public disguised as literary inefficiency by an irrational tendency to fish for public success: intuitive consciousness of greatness alternating with the desire to demonstrate himself great: unique comprehension of the possibilities of action, thought, philosophy, literature, poetry, obscured behind a mask of vagueness and indecision and irrelevancy and propriety and moans about 'wasted talents': genius obscured by the characteristics of mediocrity.

But it is only the husk which obscures, all unimportant, unless, because this outward husk is too obtrusive, the fruit is forgotten.

. . . we know nothing of ourselves, till we know *ourselves* to be as nothing.[1]

[1] 655.

4

JOINT AUTHORSHIP

To know Coleridge, in other words, it is necessary to unknow S.T.C.

In the Coleridge writings there are two authors: a 'Coleridge' to be assimilated, and an S.T.C. to be marked, noted, and, finally, skipped. Some of these notes suggest new categories, arising from this distinction, into which Coleridge's work, far more naturally than into 'prose and poetry,' or 'early and late,' falls apart.

Published and Posthumous.

'For publication' or 'not for publication' is one of these. The estecean qualities are more marked in the first: 'Coleridge' stands out in notes, letters, and marginalia. A first generalisation on this theme must be that Coleridge was too conscious of his reader; or (connected with this) that Coleridge was in the habit of assigning special importance, like a child, to something written for publication. To emphasise a point he would sometimes refer to a mythical 'essay on the subject,' which he was 'half way through.'[1] For the

[1] 688.

solemn occasion of publication, he would alter pregnant notes into something more formal, more circumlocutory; more general, less particular.

Nearly all the estecean characteristics are of the kind likely to hamper a professional author. Chief among these is the lack of psychological grace in the superficial side of his relationships, the clumsy lack of give and take in the first advances of friendship. This is reflected in an absence of humane manners towards his readers. He is always trying to remedy it, always trying to ingratiate himself, and almost always failing.

The first examples of this which occur to me are letters—but letters akin to published work because written for an occasion. Coleridge must be the worst occasional writer that ever lived. His letters of thanks for important loans, for instance. He always—that is, on three or four occasions—talks of tears, and of sitting back and musing on generosity as a fact of life before he remembers to think of the money, etc. It all reads badly; instead of simplicity there is a chilling excess of feeling. Or take the letters written to Wedgwood, his benefactor, from Germany. To show that he is not wasting his time, he goes into an encyclopædic account of the history of the Germans, with quotations from Tacitus, etc. Or the letter to the Royal Society, suggesting an impossibly learned thesis on the occasion of their reward to him.

. . . 2. The influences of the Institutions and Theology of the Latin Church on Philosophy, Language, Science and the Liberal Arts from the viith to the xiv Century.

Then, in the famous published books, there is a strong defensive quality, which has nothing whatever to do with 'Coleridge' yet which all readers of Coleridge know well—so well that Hazlitt could say in an amusing review of the newly announced *title* of *The Statesman's Manual*, that 'one could tell what anything from Coleridge would be as well before as after publication.' The controlling impulse seems to be the desire to present himself as favourably as possible, and to discountenance familiar accusations. 'I am no mystic . . .' he seems to be saying. 'I am no Jacobin . . . no Lake Poet . . . no fanatic for simplicity in verse . . . not a vague philosopher. But a reasonable man, and a good man.' He feels that he must plead a case; and attempts to get the reader on his side by some kind of emotional appeal. From *Conciones ad Populum* onwards this tone prevails; it is most obvious in the *Friend*, archetype of unsaleable periodical, and in *Biographia*, which, with all its important merits, is the most estecean publication of Coleridge. The *Friend* is the type of a book written by a man with an unconscious hatred of publication. Dorothy Wordsworth describes how parts of it were composed very rapidly—and then long, costive pauses. 'He has written a whole *Friend* more than once in two days—and then sits for days together without writing a word.' And a 'whole *Friend*' did not mean a complete essay, but so many thousand words, enough to make up a slice of the required thickness, with no relation to the general form of the work.

The *Biographia* is explicitly an apologia. He calls it an 'exculpation' on the first page, and in a letter to Frere says that his chief purpose is 'to defend myself . . . from the often and public denunciation of having wasted my time in idleness.' But the defence part of it has neither simplicity nor dignity. Its style seems partly due to a dogmatisation of his own 'Second Characteristic of Genius'—'the choice of subjects very remote from the private interests and circumstances of the writer himself.'[1] He generalises, he makes large statements—'From my first entrance into life, I have, with few and short intervals, lived either abroad or in retirement.'[2] 'Indignation at literary wrongs I leave to men born under happier stars. I cannot *afford* it.'[3] And then, all grandeur dropped, he sweeps into a swinging grievance, with particular attacks, names—Jeffrey, and then suddenly Hazlitt—often in sentences 'relegated to footnotes,' but footnotes which mysteriously seem to have become the foundation of the page. He is pleading even in the famous passages, the assessments, so that not only is the praise of Southey invalidated, but we can even understand Wordsworth saying that his own praises as sung in the *Biographia* gave him no pleasure. The prevailing tone, as distinct from the single spurts, has something of the phrase Coleridge used when he was criticising Wordsworth—'mental bombast.'

When Coleridge is not writing for publication, all is different. What he says of his notebooks applies— 'they are my only *full* confidants.'[4] He recommends

<hr>

[1] 255.   [2] 225.   [3] 221.   [4] *L.*, 597.

the study of past notebooks to men who wish to study their past selves, and speaks of 'the liveliness with which you will so often have expressed yourself in your private notebooks, in which the words, unsought for and untrimmed because intended for your own eye, exclusively, were the first-born of your first impressions.' In these notes almost all such estecean qualities as pomposity of diction, pleading, presenting himself in the character of a misunderstood man, are missing. The scrappier the piece of paper, the less abundant and virginal the margin on which he was writing, the more hazardous the chance of his note being seen again by human eye, then the more personal, penetrating, and truly autobiographical the note. In letters he is equally predisposed to true Coleridgean expressions. He only rarely—when, for instance, he is writing to a benefactor, such as Gillman or Wedgwood—writes with the publication paralysis on him. It is obvious that he never has in mind the possibility of the posthumous publication of his letters: on the contrary, he often pleads for their destruction, sending some self- or thought-description *'for you only'*: all is written with the spontaneity of the notes and marginalia. And remember, when reading letter MSS., that the words squeezed as an afterthought across a corner, or the concertinaed lines of a postscript, should be the last to be skipped.

It would be worth making a collation of parallel passages from published and unpublished wordings of thoughts. I suggest as a start the comparison of some quotation from the seventh lecture of the 1811–12 series, which was delivered in his best public manner, with some of his cogent little notes on the same subject (*Romeo and Juliet*): for example, on the Nurse—this from the lecture, with its contemplative die-away:

> Thus, in the Nurse you have all the garrulity of old age, and all its fondness; for the affection of old age is one of the greatest consolations of humanity. I have often thought what a melancholy world this would be without children, and what an inhuman world without the aged. (356)

compared with this note.

> In the garrulity of age, observe the mode of connecting by accidents of time and place, and the childlike fondness of repetition in her child[ish] age—and that happy, humble ducking under, yet resurgence against the check—
>
> 'Yes, madam! yet I cannot choose but laugh.' (369)

And study the phrasing of the note: 'What is it that I employ my metaphysics on? To perplex our clearest notions and living moral instincts?'[1] where it is redressed for publication purposes in the *Friend* (para. 1 of Introductory Essay xv). Or compare Coleridge writing to Poole a set letter for the great occasion of the first experience of fatherhood:

> When I first saw the child, I did not feel that thrill and overflowing of affection which I expected. I looked on it with a melancholy gaze; my mind was intensely contemplative and my heart only sad. (563)

[1] 163.

with a quick reminiscence in a later conversation where he mentions the Holy Infants in Dutch paintings which look 'just like the little rabbits we fathers have all seen with some dismay at first burst.'[1]

The unpremeditated Coleridge is the best Coleridge; the unprepared lecture was the most effective lecture; and the Table Talk—as Coleridge himself improvised it, not as his nephew rounded it off, or as Crabb Robinson dryly compressed it—was nearly the best of all. But nothing suited him quite so well as the unpremeditated, irrelevant, unsuitably situated, almost illegible, note.

*

Observe now this anomaly, a paradox to be demonstrated under the heading 'Coleridge's Prose Style.' Coleridge writes best when his style appears, by the usual standards, at its worst.

Coleridge's characteristic style is well known. The long sentences, the lack of plan, and the parentheses. Since it is not a deliberate attempt, like Lamb's Sir Thomas Brownism or Hazlitt's colloquialism, to overthrow the tyranny of the eighteenth-century period, it is what I like to think of as a non-style. That is to say, it is not a slowly evolved and carefully polished instrument, so beautiful or efficient in itself as to make its presence more insistently felt than the meaning to which it is nominally subservient; it is direct expression, a transparency through which the various Coleridges can be seen directly. Not that there is no 'Coleridge style.' There is a very definite and very

[1] 493.

bad STYLE which is especially evident in the youthful S.T.C. Phrases in a letter he wrote to Charles Lloyd's father in 1796 will do for an example. He is giving his reasons for wanting to live in the country: 'above all, because I am anxious that my children should be bred up from earliest infancy in the simplicity of peasants; the food, dress, and habits completely rustic . . . I am peculiarly delighted with the 21st verse of the 42nd chapter of Tobit . . .' 'Poole is mentioned:' 'in my rustic scheme . . . we shall reside near a very dear friend of mine, well versed from childhood in the tasks of the Garden and the Field . . .' and the possibilities of kitchen gardening: 'I shall devote my *days* to the acquirement of *practical* husbandry and horticulture. . . .'[1] The inexperienced Coleridge reader will be mystified by such passages—they occur even in *Biographia*. But they have nothing to do with Coleridge except as further examples of his inability to see any of his prose compositions objectively. Coleridge's Style, with its petrifying elegance, is an amusing aberration. His non-style, his loose structure, his way of going off into parentheses, of giving birth to a new long sentence half-way through the old one, of italicising, of writing lengthily—all this, if good writing is successful self-revelation, is the perfection of authorship.

I would defend the points of this non-style *seriatim*. If the importance of what a man has to say depends on his general drift, voluminousness is almost an essential; and it is a good safeguard against the mistake of looking for the epitomisable in Coleridge. He is

[1] E.V.L., 31.

responsible for only one epigram.[1] He had too much to say to write for effect. As an excuse for his habit of talking at length, he would explain that his thought accumulated when he was alone so that he longed to pour it forth. But why, when it came to writing them down, should not Coleridge have delivered these thoughts more succinctly, with greater art of clarity? Clarity was his motive. Coleridge knew, and hated, all the gambits of the readable writer. He liked to mark them in the controversial books he read, and is awake to well-concealed rhetorical dodges meant to deceive the reader. Up against an 'effectively' balanced shaft against Sabbatarianism:

> [The same religious abstinence from all appearance of recreation on the Lord's day; and the same neglect of the weightier matters of the moral law, in the course of the week,]

he writes:

> This sentence thus smuggled in at the bottom of the chest ought not to pass unnoticed; for the whole force of the former depends on it. It is a true trick, and deserves reprobation. (*L.R.*, iv. 368)

He especially derides mechanical uses of the period, such as the easy device of getting through a long sentence by the repetition of 'that he . . . that he' or 'a man who . . . a man who,' etc. He thinks it the result of hurried writing, and complains of the 'isochronous asthmatic pants' of 'He—he—he—he.'[2]

---

[1] Summer sets in with its usual severity.   [2] *L.*, 506.

Speaking of Junius as type of the incisive-effective writer, in perfect command of such devices as the occasional induction of startling facts, lively illustrations and witty applications of good stories, etc., Coleridge says that such writing is essential for those who would wish 'to be the important and long-remembered agent of a faction.'[1] He believes, he says, that he himself could write in this way if he could have aims of this sort—'But it is not in my nature. I not only love truth, but I have a passion for the legitimate investigation of the truth.' In short, he does not want to make his point by psychological devices— hyperbole, period, etc. (his very fault in his estecean moments). He wants all his words to have a true bearing on his meaning. And that is what he achieves. That is why it is impossible ever to slide or to skim when reading Coleridge, to say 'yes' before the end of the sentence has arrived. For his cadences will never finish according to the rules of mechanical balance, but are in contact with a gradually disentangling meaning to the end, or may be broken, as Coleridge turns to consult himself once again on the precise value of a word, the exact reason for a train of thought. Praising the quietness of Leighton's style, Coleridge makes his comment on the effectiveness of ineffectiveness. 'Sacrifice of particular effects . . . wonderfully facilitating the soft and quiet *illapse* [of his meaning] into the very recesses of our conviction.'[2] For 'Archbishop Leighton's style' the reader will tacitly substitute 'Coleridge's style.'

[1] 422.   [2] *L.,* 718.

Coleridge's chief sin against schoolbook prose lies in the length and frequency of his parentheses. Coleridge laughs at himself for them—'Excuse my long digression,' he says, and: 'How shall I get out of this sentence?'[1] For he has a conscious as well as an unconscious motive. Unconsciously, there were psychological reasons which made Coleridge able to write more freely when he was not sticking to the subject enunciated in his title. Consciously, Coleridge liked to discuss with himself *why* his thoughts had taken a certain trend, his arguments a certain shape. Sentences with brackets are the last which experienced Coleridge readers skip. As Crabb Robinson said of his lectures, 'those hearers who enjoyed him most probably enjoyed most his digressions.' Coleridge himself gives us the root-of-roots answer if we combine a letter of 1816 with one of 1810:

'A book of reasoning without parentheses must be the work either of adeptship or of a *pliable* intellect.'[2]

The explanation:

Of parentheses I may be too fond, and will be on my guard in this respect. But I am certain that no work of impassioned and eloquent reasoning ever did or could subsist without them. They are the drama of reason, and present the thought growing, instead of a mere Hortus siccus. The aversion to them is one of the numberless symptoms of a feeble Frenchified Public (631).

Coleridge's style, then, is not clear in the sense that the meaning of the words can be taken in at a glance,

[1] 660.　　　　[2] 665.

nor in the sense that an argument is skilfully and incisively demonstrated. But his terms have that triplefold lucidity in which the word is a clear expression of a thought which is itself 'original'—*i.e.* a clear reflection of 'Coleridge'; word=thought=identity of the author: the difficulties arise from Coleridge's refusal to make clear from the outside thoughts which take their clarity from inside.

Coleridge seeks for the word. Not like Johnson (whom he would have liked, *a propos* his influence on prose style, to have cut to the liver) for the Latinate word, nor like Lamb for the seventeenth-century word, nor even for the delightfully inevitable word, the 'final' word, but for the seminative word, the word which the reader can interpret fruitfully only if he himself is fallow ground.

This is the key. Coleridge is famous for a strong grasp of the principles of rhythmically constructed verse. Sometimes, in verses, he expresses truth in the beauty of his cadences alone. But in prose he is anxious not for the sound of the sentence, but the meaning of the word. Readers of Coleridge soon begin to find that for them the word 'word' is changing. They realise that for Coleridge 'the word' is alive. 'Language,' he says, 'is often inadequate, sometimes deficient, but never false or delusive.'[1] From his first boyhood he investigated the meaning of every word, and the reason of its choice and position. But words not only 'as far as relates to speaking, but the knowledge of words as distinct component parts, which we

[1] 460.

learn by learning to read.'[1] And with this a love of words, particularly of single words—*e.g.* 'the *word* "homogeneous" gives me great pleasure.'[2]

But 'objective interest in words' would be a misleading phrase here. It sounds like a philological interest only (a side-interest which in fact was present also). The printed word for Coleridge has a depth dimension, a root, so that his distinctions, for instance, are less than any other writer's merely verbal. He will take a word like 'Reason,' or 'Idea,' and create into it the meaning of an individual experience, really using the word, not letting it use him, giving the word itself life (tending to choose dead, sapless words for his purpose), so that instead of confining meaning, fixing it, he implants a seed of meaning, capable of growth.

Once the importance of words to Coleridge is understood, the reader will see Coleridge's preoccupation with them everywhere. His assertion that 'not the least important' object of the *Biographia* was to settle the poetic diction controversy, and his giving as his first reason for writing *Aids to Reflection* the desire to direct his readers' attention to the 'value of the Science of Words, their use and abuse, and the incalculable advantages attached to the habit of using them appropriately, and with a distinct knowledge of their primary, derivative, and metaphorical senses.' Then from the body of his work—his 'Romantic Revival' prejudice against the eighteenth century takes the form of an attack on the casual and arbitrary *phraseology* of its writers. Or compare his

[1] *A.P.*, 11. [2] 598.

hatred of public playing about with language, of making puns out of famous phrases—*e.g.* 'to wed or not to wed,'[1] and similar defilements. 'It shows a base and unpoetical mind to convert so beautiful, so divine a subject as language into the vehicle or make-weight of political squibs.'[2]

In his own choice of words he seems less careful than he is, being typically innocent of any technique of sincerity, of the effectiveness of under-statement, and so on. But he is justified in saying of himself that there are few writers who choose their words more carefully;[3] or in adding as signature to a carefully worded thought:

> There is not one word I would add or withdraw from this, scarcely one which I would substitute. (480)

He attacks the 'vicious phraseology'[4] which he says he meets everywhere—sermons, newspapers, after-dinner speeches: no dangerous facility of phrase will he let pass, writing in the margin against a too breezy definition of a miracle:

> Suspension of the laws of nature! suspension—laws—nature! Bless me! a chapter would be required for the explanation of each several word of this definition, and little less than omniscience for its application in any one instance. (*L.R.*, iv. 276)

He is quick to name and isolate verbal irritations of which we are only half-conscious—*e.g.* the intro-

[1] 672.   [2] 488.   [3] 174.   [4] 292.

duction of proper names of the kind which need notes for explanation. 'Unknown names,' he says, 'are non-conductors: they stop all sympathy.'[1] And Coleridge's care with words is always that of a poet, never that of a pedant. It is almost a principle with him, for instance, not to make a correct quotation; on the other hand, some of his misquotations are more like the originals than the originals themselves. His version of an *Amoretti* sonnet in *B.L.*, ii. 150, if he had been only a little more courageous in taking liberties, might have illustrated the characteristics of the whole sequence.[2]

There is a special boldness with words which Coleridge often indulges in letters and notes, but which S.T.C. gravely eliminates for publication purposes. Good word inventions, like 'day-mair';[3] unallowable adjectives: 'the cadaverous silence of Godwin's children is to me quite catacombish'; unorthodox metaphors —*e.g.* for philosophical arguments against a religious tenet:

Besides, how childish to puff up the empty bladder of an old meta-physical foot-ball on the *modus operandi interior* of Justification into a shew of practical substance; as if it were no less solid than a cannon ball! Why, drive it with all the vehemence that five toes can exert, it would not kill a louse on the head of Methodism. (*L.R.*, iv. 336)

Similes: 'as plain as a whale's foal, or Sarah Robarts's rabbits.'[4] And some language-gala hyperboles. 'A

[1] 334.   [2] *Cf.* note, 763.
[3] MS. Add,, 35, 343. f. 127.   [4] *L.R.*, iv. 338.

tall old Hag, whose soul-gelding ugliness would chill to eternal chastity a cantharidized Satyr.'[1] On Beaumont and Fletcher's *Maid in the Mill*:

> a woman must not merely have grown old in brothels, but have chuckled over every abomination committed in them with a rampant sympathy of imagination, to have had her fancy so drunk with the *minutiæ* of lechery as this icy chaste virgin evinces hers to have been. (410)

Descriptive phrases. A 'tobacco-toothed parson.' Or, contrasting, I think now of a letter (*L.*, 433) with a perfectly descriptive phrase for Hartley, Derwent, and Sara respectively, the words of it plain and powerful —as in this for Dorothy Wordsworth: 'Her manners are simple, ardent, impressive. In every motion, her most innocent soul outbeams so brightly.' *Cf.* this, for a storm on the Kirkstone:

> I am no novice in storms; but such as this I never before witnessed, combining the violence of the wind and rain with the intensity of the cold. My hands were shrivelled like a washerwoman's and the rain was pelted or rather slung, by the wind against my face, like splinters of flint and seemed to *cut* my flesh. On turning the mountain at the first step of descent all was calm and breathless. It seemed as if there was a great fountain of wind and tempest on the summit that rolled down a Niagara of air towards Patterdale. (*U.L.*, i. 242)

We have fought shy of Coleridge's neologisms.

[1] 557.

'Pantisocracy,' 'Aspheterize,' 'Esemplastic' have failed. He is responsible for the re-introduction of the word 'sensuous'—(*cf. N.E.D.*). But on the whole he does not seem to have had much effect on vocabulary. Perhaps this is as well, because such a word as 'enucleation' has one depth of significance as used by Coleridge, quite another as used by somebody else. Coleridge did not depend on the arresting phrase, detachable from its context. On the contrary, he used words of vague definition and wide application—in philosophy often using venerable and familiar words —but giving them meaning by virtue of the fact that he himself had a life, a development, to give to his sentences a new and individual drift.

It is very estecean that Coleridge should have missed his *obvious* opportunity of demonstrating some of those mysteries to his contemporaries—by writing what he was so much more competent to write than Wordsworth, the preface to the *Lyrical Ballads*. Such a site was altogether too propitious to attract Coleridge. He prefers to make us rout out, as it were, these invaluable dicta from the bottom of the dustbin.

Criticism.

Coleridge has popular fame as a critic not because he is confident and daring in his criticism, original, and able to grasp his subject nearer the root than any of his contemporaries: all this applies equally well to Coleridge On Religion, Ethics, etc. The reason is that Coleridge never wrote a specifically critical book. Because he never associated criticism with his *magnum opus* mood, S.T.C. is in abeyance. Coleridge, who had the power and the justification to praise, was occasionally eulogistic merely—of Wordsworth, or Shakespeare. In his longing for sympathy he had a natural tendency to praise those who praised him—such as J. H. Frere: but it is very slight. And because he has no undivine detachment, Coleridge tends to surround with an aura those with whom some step in his evolution is associated, in honour of the happy experience—Bowles, for instance, or Hartley. And he would not print the bathotic 'Next to the inspired Scriptures . . . stands Leighton's Commentary on the first Epistle of Peter'[1] if the reading of Leighton had not happened to coincide with some unfolding of his own consciousness. Of uncritical antagonistic judgments I can only think of one—a remarkable expression, surely, of a subjugated feeling of bitterness against Wordsworth—when in the *Biographia*, speaking of Wordsworth's *Ode on the Intimations of Immortality* and his 'best philosopher. . . . Haunted for ever by the Eternal Mind,' he remarks that 'Children at this age give us no such information of themselves.'[2]

An example of the pitfalls of judgment without sympathy—from the great exponent of the prime necessity of sympathy before right judgment is possible. A good introduction to Coleridge's criticism would be to handle the actual copy of the volume which Coleridge himself had read. 'I read all sorts of books with

[1] 196.
[2] Since the above was written, Mr. Richards' interesting analysis of this criticism has appeared.

some pleasure,' he says, 'except modern sermons and treatises on political economy.'[1] As a critic he did not read critically. He attacked books, breaking down the detachment of print, en-Coleridging them with under-linings and comments written over the margins, borrowing books, most often, and sending them back after too long delay with too many physical signs that meaning had been wrung from them by the Cole-ridge onslaught. And the comments are generally to mark an argument, or suggest an enlargement. Cole-ridge seems to be 'with' the writer. He is reading not for criticism and ideas, not with a self-limiting, but with a self-finding purpose.

Result—a constructive criticism. Coleridge dog-matises it thus. In criticism, 'the wise is the genial.'[2] In criticism, 'never to admit the *faults* of a work of genius to those who denied or were incapable of feeling and understanding the *beauties*.'[3] 'The genial judgment is to distinguish accurately the character and characteristics of each poem, praising them accord-ing to . . . their own kind'[2]—to identify yourself with the writer, that is. ('To have an exclusive pleasure in poetry, not being yourself a poet . . . is an un-worthy and effeminate thing.') In short, it is Cole-ridge's constant purpose 'never to lose an opportunity of reasoning against the head-dimming, heart-damping principle of judging a work by its defects, not its beauties.'

The wise is the genial. Heaven knows what special significance of context or derivation Coleridge is giving

[1] 518.   [2] *M.*   [3] *L.*, 697.

the word. But he does not mean 'kindly.' He is dogmatising from his own power of relating some potential quality in himself to the essential quality of his subject, so that he is strictly compassionate, so that he has the fullest things to say of the strengths of the greatest writers—Cervantes, Defoe, Shakespeare. He can criticise Rabelais in terms of Rabelais' human splendour, Milton in terms of Milton's qualified integrity, Luther in terms of Luther's simplicity, etc., disagreeing on a detail only or application of a point ('Nay, but dear honoured Luther!' . . . 'Oh that the dear man Luther had but told us here what he meant by the term[1] . . .'), but in sympathy with the general purpose.

'Sympathy' is a dangerous word—it is perhaps not the right word. Coleridge was able, as he evolved, to render each of his various souls more conscious and more active by absorbing the souls of others. It is something more active, then, than sympathy. 'Meditate often on these truths, that they may become your feelings.' Perhaps 'incorporation' gives it. In some such word lies the explanation of the power of Coleridge's criticism. Readers soon notice how much of his commentaries read like self-description, more unreservedly autobiographical, even, than when he is talking directly about himself. I can think of a few scattered examples, and one obvious one. Miscellaneous: He criticises Southey's Life of Bunyan because Southey did not illustrate 'That mood of mind which exaggerates, and still more, mistakes, the inward depravation, as in

[1] L.R., iv. 8 ff.

Bunyan, Nelson, and others, by extracts from Baxter's *Life of himself.*[1] Coleridge reads himself into revelations of morbid states of conscience. The margins of his copy of Baxter's *Life* are full of sympathetic comments. 'What a picture of myself,' he will say.[2] At random—on Jeremy Taylor. His 'discursive intellect dazzle-darkened his intuition.'[3] His best writing is in 'the digressions, overgrowths, parenthetic *obiter et in transitu* sentences.'[4] On Milton's style: 'Every word is to the purpose. There are no lazy intervals. . . . If this be called obscurity, let it be remembered that it is such an obscurity as is a compliment to the reader. . . .'[5] What pictures of Coleridge's style!

As texts for this—Coleridge on reading Leighton: 'I identify myself with the excellent writer, and his thoughts become my thoughts.'[6] Or Coleridge on reading Sir Thomas Browne: 'I have never read a book in which I feel greater similarity to my own make of mind. . . .'[7]

The best example to study would be Coleridge's criticism of Shakespeare. The fact of 'Coleridge, the great Shakespeare critic,' is rather difficult for us to realise now that we grow up with Coleridge's Shakespeare part of our culture, a familiar piece of intellectual furniture. Nor is it difficult to be critical, to notice estecean signs, if we read the Shakespearean criticism in bulk (in the unselected collection of Professor Raysor). Esteceanism in the moral disapproval which is illogically at the back of his subtlest diagnosis of

---

[1] 489.   [2] *L.R.*, iv. 81.   [3] 659.
[4] 464.   [5] 415.   [6] *L.R.*, iv. 172.   [7] 414.

villainy (Iago 'next to devil'). In his praise for the
piety of Shakespeare, saying that unlike Beaumont
and Fletcher he is always respectful to the Church.
In his upset over the 'low porter soliloquy' of Macbeth,
and his inability to see Shakespeare's liking for Edmund
whose 'shame' in illegitimacy appears to Coleridge to
be made particularly unbearable by Gloucester's
confession 'that he was at the time [of Edmund's
begetting] a married man.'

The prime fact—that Coleridge was the first Shakespeare critic, in the positive sense—is passed over: and
it is *because* the Shakespeare of our generation is, to a
measurable extent, Shakespeare plus Coleridge.

Coleridge made the first addition. Before his time
there had been blank admiration, expressive, as Coleridge says, of 'the most vulgar of all feelings, wonder-
ment.' There had been textual criticism; eloquent
phrases, from Dryden and others. Straightforward
catalogues of merits and demerits by Dr. Johnson,
from the detached common-sense point of view—
lessenings, essentially. And towards the end of the
century, interesting analyses of single characters—
Falstaff, and Richard II. For the rest, comments on
the great by the small, uneasily conscious of the
necessity of coming up to scratch for the great
occasion.

Every critic, who has or has not made a collection
of black letter books—in itself a useful and respect-
able amusement—puts on the seven-league boots
of self-opinion and strides at once from an illustrator
into a supreme judge, and blind and deaf, fills his

three-ounce phial at the waters of Niagara—and
determines positively the greatness of the cataract
to be neither more nor less than his three-ounce
phial has been able to receive. (345)

With Coleridge, the reading of Shakespeare is
scarcely dissociable from increase of consciousness.
As he evolves, he knows Shakespeare better. If there
are lines he does not understand, he says (with perfect
sincerity): 'I cherish the hope that I am mistaken and,
becoming wiser, shall discover some profound excellence in what I now appear to myself to detect an
imperfection.'[1] And the special part of himself which
he becomes aware of through Shakespeare is his
psychological complexity, and the root of essential
unity from which the complexity springs. No one will
ever go beyond Coleridge in the demonstration of this
aspect of Shakespeare, though some have done much
to complete the extension of his demonstration in the
same plane—Bradley on Cleopatra and Falstaff, for
instance, characters which Coleridge perhaps neglected in deference to the feelings of S.T.C. In Coleridge alone it is a new criticism, because only with
Coleridge is it a reflection of the achievements, the
frustrations, and the power of differentiation of his own
personality. Because of its reflection in himself, Coleridge can demonstrate the truth of the psychology in
Shakespeare just as he is made instantly aware of a
mistake—as for instance when Shakespeare makes
Autolycus finish off his opening soliloquy with:

[1] 400.

139

. . . for the life to come, I sleep
out the thought of it.

'Too Macbeth-like,' says Coleridge, 'in the "snapper-
up of unconsidered trifles." '

'Too Hamlet-like,' a critic suggests that Coleridge
should have said. But Hamlet's was another kind of
despair, according to Coleridge, who since he discovered himself more completely in Hamlet than in
any other subject of his criticism cannot with precision
be said to be wrong in his judgments on this character.

'I have a smack of Hamlet myself, if I may say so,'
says S.T.C. somewhere, not without satisfaction.
The parallel must frequently have been noted. A
'Coleridge and S.T.C.' problem is so clearly the problem of Hamlet. It seemed sometimes to Coleridge's
friends that when he was speaking of Hamlet he was
speaking of himself. It seemed so to Crabb Robinson.

> Last night he concluded his fine development of
> the Prince of Denmark by an eloquent statement of
> the moral of the play: 'Action,' he said, 'is the great
> end of all. No intellect, however grand, is valuable
> if it draw us from action and lead us to think and
> think till the time of action is passed by and we can
> do nothing.' Somebody said to me, 'This is a satire
> on himself.'—'No,' said I, 'it is an elegy.' A great
> many of his remarks on Hamlet were capable of a
> like application. (*S.C.*, ii. 229)

Many of Coleridge's observations on Hamlet actually
echo phrases he uses elsewhere in the description of

himself, especially when he is concentrating on Hamlet's heterogeneity, and the causes of his inaction. Compare a lecture:

[Shakespeare in his character of Hamlet] intended to pourtray a person, in whose view the external world, and all its incidents and objects, were comparatively dim, and of no interest in themselves, and which began to interest only, when they were reflected in the mirror of his mind. (*S.C.*, ii. 129)

With a letter to Mrs. Coleridge on himself:

I seem to exist, as it were, almost wholly within myself, in *thoughts* rather than in *things*, in a particular warmth felt *all* over me, but chiefly felt about my head and breast; and am connected with *things without me* by the pleasurable sense of their immediate Beauty or Loveliness, and not at all by my knowledge of the average value of the minds of people in general. (597)

Or another lecture:

Hamlet . . . is called upon to act by every motive human and divine, but the great object of his life is defeated by continually resolving to do, yet doing nothing but resolve. (*S.C.*, ii. 198)

With another letter on himself:

MY DEAR MORGAN,—Tomorrow morning, I doubt not, I shall be of clear and collected Spirits; but tonight I feel that I should do nothing to any purpose, but and excepting Thinking, Planning, and

Resolving to resolve—and praying to be able to execute. (648)

The mere placing of Hamlet soliloquies in a Coleridge context is a mutual illumination. Further, Coleridge describes himself in noting certain miscellaneous detail. He is interested in Hamlet's word-play: he notes that 'the digressions and enlargements consist of reflections, truths, and principles of general and permanent interest': notes again that 'every incident sets him thinking.' Perfect Coleridge—like the realisation that it was not doubt as to the right course of action which troubled Hamlet.[1] Coleridge-Hamlet was made impotent by a faculty of motive knowing, of principle possession, so developed as to be hopelessly out of proportion greater than his power of translation into action.

Even in the less directly applicable observations, when for instance Coleridge comments on Hamlet's assumed wildness after seeing the ghost:

O that subtle trick to pretend the *acting* only when we are very near *being* what we act. (140)

Even here, Coleridge seems to be half soliloquising (in the Hamlet way) on himself.

Coleridge's Hamlet epitomises the value of Coleridge as a critic. His comments expressed a relation, not a judgment; he brought out a certain quality in the writers he discussed—varying aspects and degrees of the predominating quality in himself. But Hazlitt's

[1] *S.C.*, i. 194.

gibe, that it was possible to know anything that Coleridge wrote as well before as after reading it is truer than Hazlitt knew—is Coleridge's strength, as a critic, because the Coleridge quality is radical differentiation. Once Coleridge is known, then writers or their creations can be newly differentiated merely by placing them in the Coleridge context. And it is the difference, the uniqueness, which will be made emphatic: not the consanguineity with some type.[1]

Coleridge, in short, does not judge by rules, but by a Principle, a criterion—the criterion of his own identity. He writes to his friend, Wade. How curious, he says, is the behaviour of a man of opinions, like Erasmus Darwin. *'All at once he makes up his mind* on such important subjects, as whether we be the outcasts of a blind idiot called Nature, or the children of an all-wise and infinitely good God.'[2] Coleridge, in the slow infiltration of his criticism, has no unexpected favourites, no cranky *pro*, or *anti* founded on a sudden judgment; nor is it a reflection of his character, a judgment in terms of S.T.C., in terms of his estecean ideal of himself; so that his subjects turn neither into S.T.C.'s *in excelsis*, nor S.T.C.'s *manqués*, in the manner

[1] *Cf.* p. 242 ff., where the Coleridge 'quality' is discussed. Note that the ground of Coleridge's æsthetic theory, even, has the same self-descriptiveness. How strange this theory of the origin of metre reads after eighteenth century dicta on the subject: 'I would trace it to the balance in the mind affected by that spontaneous effort which strives to hold in check the workings of passion.' A personal experience. Even his definition of beauty—'unity in multeity'—of little originality detached from its context, gains its force from the fact that the phrase describes Coleridge's ideal not only for art but for man, for himself—'homogeneity.' (*B.L.*)

[2] *L.*, 153.

so limiting to much otherwise entertaining and forceful modern criticism.

This is precisely the kind of subject on which Coleridge is fluent, and I reproduce the following as fitting seminatory matter with which to close his own statement of the problem—not because, in the lecture transcript in which it appears, it is lucid, but because it is profound, the deepest probe into the subject.

Shakespeare shaped his characters out of the nature within; but we cannot so safely say, out of his own nature as an individual person. No! this latter is itself but a *natura naturata*,—an effect, a product, not a power. It was Shakespeare's prerogative to have the universal, which is potentially in each particular, opened out to him, the *homo generalis*, not as an abstraction from observation of a variety of men, but as the substance capable of endless modifications, of which his own personal existence was but one, and to use this one as the eye that beheld the other, and as the tongue that could convey the discovery. There is no greater or more common vice in dramatic writers than to draw out of themselves. (347)

Than to draw, that is, out of their set and circumscribing characters. Coleridge understood this power in Shakespeare, because he possessed it himself. He did not summarise men from the surface plane of his character, but knew them from the source from which all differentiation springs, obscure because central. I know of no quotation better exemplifying Coleridge—

the outward difficulty, because of the inward clarity, the radical clarity, of the thought.

Verse.

Why so violent against *metaphysics* in poetry?

Is Coleridge ever, in his poetry, Coleridge entire? If his verse were to be judged by its average examples, which would be absurd, it could be said that Coleridge in his verse was Coleridge elegant. If it were to be judged by the group of poems specially qualified for mention in literary histories, it could be said that Coleridge here was Romantic Revivalist. Could it also be said, with reference to the six or seven great poems, that here is Coleridge feeling, or here is Coleridge marvellously language-orchestrating—*only?*

In the *Song of the Answerer*, Whitman, in his enormous manner, enunciates. He distinguishes the poet of exquisite sound only, 'the singer,' from 'the true poet.'

The singers do not beget, only the Poet begets,
The singers are welcomed, understood, appear
    often enough, but rarely has the day been,
    likewise the spot, of the birth of the maker of
    poems, the Answerer . . .
The name of the singer is, eye-singer, ear-
    singer, head-singer, sweet-singer, night-singer,
    parlor-singer, love-singer, weird-singer, or
    something else.
All this time and at all times wait the words of
    true poems,
The words of true poems do not merely please,

> The true poets are not followers of beauty but
> the august masters of beauty; . . .
> The words of true poems are the tuft and final
> applause of science.

The greatest poetry expresses, with every degree of indirectness, a personal philosophy, of the kind which is a revaluation of the world. Coleridge created this very kind of personal philosophy, but he does not set it forth in his verse. Except for a few lines in the æsthetically crude *Religious Musings*, except for a few stanzas in the *Ode to Dejection*, it is nowhere even implicit in his verse.

Coleridge knew this: 'Why so violent against *metaphysics* in poetry?' he asks the theoretical Thelwall, who liked his poetry placid, charming: and Coleridge in 1796 considered his greatest performances, unlikely to be surpassed, the metaphysical poems *Religious Musings*, and *Destiny of Nations*, though it was a kind of metaphysic which he afterwards denominated 'so-called.'

> Even in my dawn of youth—Philosophy:
> Tho' then, unconscious of herself, pardie,
> She bore no other name than Poesy.
> <div align="right">(<i>Cf. B.L.</i>, i. xiv)</div>

Coleridge believed that the whole self must be active in the apprehension of reality, so he believed that its expression must be looked for in a poet; that 'real' philosopher and 'real' poet are interchangeable terms.

Metaphysics is a word that you, my dear sir, are no great friend to, but yet you will agree with me that a great poet must be *implicité*, if not *explicité*, a profound metaphysician. He may not have it in logical coherence in his brain and tongue, but . . . (*L.*, 372)

How may he have it? I select from many apposite contexts, for problems of this primary kind Coleridge thought out and thought out again. There is a note (*A.P.*, 96) about poets not being 'indulgers of fancy . . . they are . . . the true protoplasts . . . Gods of love who tame the chaos.' There is a letter[1] on the reverse qualities of Southey, archetype of superficial poet in his facile moments. And though Coleridge never wrote what he thought, after reading the first draft of the *Prelude*, that it was the province of Wordsworth to write—the 'first genuine philosophic poem'—there is MS. evidence that he came as near doing it as his impotence in the face of a large-scale work allowed him. In *Coleridge on Logic and Learning*[2] there is reprinted a scheme of a *magnum opus* which has the very framework of an epic poem. He speaks of it as early as 1797:

I should not think of devoting less than 20 years to an Epic Poem. Ten to collect materials and warm my mind with universal science. I would be a tolerable Mathematician, I would thoroughly know Mechanics, Hydrostatics, Optics, and Astronomy, Botany, Metallurgy, Fossilism, Chemistry, Geology, Anatomy, Medicine—then the *mind of man*—then the *minds* of *men*— (573)

[1] 573.   [2] A.D.S., 3 ff.

If the suggestion that the thorough knowledge of Fossilism is a necessary ingredient of great poetry seems like one of those thrusts which the faithful Coleridgeans find hardest to bear, I will quote further back in his letter. Coleridge has been speaking of Milton:

> Observe the march of Milton—his severe application, his laborious polish, his deep metaphysical researches, his prayers to God before he began his great poem . . .'

Coleridge himself did not write the great poem: wonderfully as some of his poems succeed, he was not successful according to his own criterion. Not that there is about his poetry as a whole too little of generality, there is too much: too much allegiance to a dogmatism of his on what a poem ought to be—a belief that it should show 'the utter *aloofness* of the poet's own feelings from those of which he is at once the painter and the analyst.'[1] Not enough respect paid to a saving corollary enunciated elsewhere:—'combine the permanent in the *individual*.' For whatever the philosophy of poetry may express, the language of that philosophy is not aloof, or abstract, but a demonstration *from the particular* of the infinite generalisations latent in that particular. This may have hindered him, or it may have been a right instinct. Complete Works did not flourish in his soil. Whatever the reason, poetry of the kind whose successive recreations of the Word he said it was the duty of criticism to trace,[2] Coleridge himself could not write.

[1] 256. [2] *Cf.* 317.

There were doubtless estecean impediments.

The sharp division of Coleridge's metrical works into beautiful poetry and indifferent verse suggests another exemplification of my main thesis. The worser half of *Poems*—the worser four-fifths if we include the original dramas—have much less merit than anything else he wrote.

The estecean element in the bad verse is strong. It follows the estecean ideal of gravity; the calm old philosopher with quiet tears upon his cheek in the later verse, the grand apostle of freedom and right in the earlier. The tone is reflected very strangely in the diction, which especially in the early verse is full of elegant abstractions and solemn words printed in capitals—'printer's devils' capitals' as Coleridge called them.[1] Almost alone in these bad verses Coleridge's quick perception of the value of words is lost.

In these verses, also, we are reminded of our knowledge that Coleridge lived in the age of the Romantic Revival. Pioneers of romance are of course at their least good when they are being pioneers of romance, and the romantic convention, though Coleridge could transcend it, had a fatal fascination for S.T.C. It suited the estecean ideal of the Poet, of the Liberator, of the 'choice of subject remote,' etc. How the convention hampered him can be worked out in detail by anyone who compares romantic early and de-romanticised late texts. Stock examples are the first and last texts of *Love*, the first and last texts of *The Ancient Mariner*. Even the climax of his poetry, the

---

[1] *Cf.* C.'s estecean alterations to poor Charles Lamb's early verses.

final version of *The Ancient Mariner*, seems to me not quite free from S.T.C. Is not the Watts-like sentiment at the end an estecean addition?

> He prayeth best who loveth best
> All things both great and small. . . .

A smooth and lovely sound—but as moral to the *Rime*? Did the reader dream he had been bathing in the reviving horrors of the nameless seas of *Moby Dick*, he is suddenly reminded that the poem was written within walking distance of a Unitarian Chapel. For the moral has no connection with the poem—is even quite inadequate to explain the symbolism of the falling of the albatross from the mariner's neck (when he *saw*, when he *apprehended*). The power of *The Ancient Mariner* is wonderfully removed from the gravities of S.T.C. At its best it bends the romantic convention to its own service as grandly as *Hamlet* employs ghost and usurpation themes. But the moral . . . Mrs. Barbauld once complained (it is recorded in *Table Talk*) that there was 'not enough moral in *The Ancient Mariner*.' On the contrary, Coleridge replied, there is too much. Perhaps this is what he meant.

'Coleridge' is in the poems then, but rarely. He is in the self-knowledge of the *Ode*: the poems of 1797–9 are the outward evidence of his experience from nature. His purest self-expression, some may feel, lies in the sound-and-rhythm units of his verse—*e.g.* the paragraph of *Christabel* beginning 'Is the night chilly and dark?' As Coleridge says, 'the sense of musical delight, with the power of producing it, is a gift of the imagination.'[1] He declaims at length on examples of this power in single lines of his own poems.[2] Thus early I have come to the end of all that seems pertinent to the title of my work under heading *Verse*. Except to point out that Coleridge was truly modest in his claims to be a poet. He once charmed Keats by talking of his poetry, and adding: 'If there is anything I have written which may be *called* poetry.' This without affectation. And in 1802 he says: 'As to myself, all my poetic genius (if ever I really possessed any *genius*, and it was not rather a mere general *aptitude* of talent, and a quickness in imitation) is gone.'[3] This in complete sincerity. He mentions his poems only rarely, and then it is of the philosophical poems he most often talks—there are in the letters frequent quotations from the *Ode*. But of his earlier verse he speaks most frequently in excuse. A young man 'has such a high idea of what poetry ought to be that he cannot conceive that such things as his natural emotions may be allowed to find a place in it. . . .'[4] hence ' all his powers of buckram are put on the stretch.' He may have felt about his early verse as he felt when he read Chatterton's:—on a life and death so full of heart-going *realities* as poor Chatterton's, to find such shadowy nobodies as cherub-winged *Death*, Trees of *Hope*, barebosomed *Affection*, and simpering *Peace*, makes one's blood circulate like ipecacuanha.'

Coleridge believed more in his power of criticism,

[1] 255.   [2] C., i. 138.
[3] L., 388.   [4] 574.

which meant his power of forming relations: of Wordsworth he says:—'I feel myself a better poet, in knowing how to honour *him* than in all my poetic compositions, all I have done or hope to do. . . .'[1]

A right intuition. Coleridge knew *persons*, could honour persons, a rarer and better gift even than the power of fascinating the world with word music.

[1] 613.

5

TRIANGULAR FRIENDSHIP

WHEN we find ourselves as educated in the expression of our emotions as we are in the history, causes, and comparative anatomy of them: when we begin to know the possibilities, the extent and kind of the fusions incident to the mutual explorations of men, when our capacity for relationship is greater, then will be studied, with more seminative results, the friendships of men like Coleridge.

Coleridge possessed the prime qualification for friendship. He made his own world—his morality, religion, standards, were all special to himself. He had a world ready to fuse with another's. For the purpose of his own evolution, he needed this kind of fertilisation. He had the right to wonder, as he did, why differences should be linked with hatred.[1]

So it is not surprising, as those who have read the Coleridge-Southey letters or the Coleridge-Wordsworth letters will know, that friendship with him was never a matter of nicely inarticulate communion, of mutual head-scratching, but an attack, with no preliminary fencing and nothing of reticence about it. Each friendship was a separate experience.

[1] 160.

If friends are friends, Coleridge says, a man lives with each a several and individual life.[1] And once the experience of such friendship has been absorbed, there is no static amiable period. The give-and-take of discovery is over, and the friendship ends. The respective characters of the participants, too long unhumoured, take their revenge. There is a quarrel. New relationships are sought.

Coleridge's life with each of his friends, therefore, starts with a flare-up of enthusiastic outpouring, and ends in a way which to the cold eye of loyalty seems reprehensible. Friendship through the ordinary approaches of mutual interests, etc., though it attracted him, he was not made for. There had to be a self-changing element; if not a reciprocation of worlds, then at any rate some kind of discipleship.

So that Coleridge was born to be disliked by the man finally formed and set, or the self-defensive man, who had nothing to give and who could receive nothing, and who regarded Coleridge askance as a preacher. Such men (with all their tempting qualities) would be Hazlitt, or Jeffrey, whose antipathies to Coleridge are known. It is natural that Hazlitt should see in Coleridge's history nothing more than a crescendo of estecean faults. And from Coleridge's side it was impossible for him to be the friend of a man like, say, Sam Rogers, wit and social figure, or Sir James Mackintosh, with his urbane sympathy from behind impermeable defences. Coleridge expresses a rare antipathy towards both these men. Nor

[1] 185.

could he have much contact with such a self-deceiver, however generous, admiring, and well-intentioned, as Cottle. Coleridge is dissecting all such antitypes to himself when he describes Lloyd, the author of *State Worthies*:

> I have a mind to draw a complete character of a worldly-wise man out of Lloyd. He would be highly-finished, useful, honoured, popular—a man revered by his children, his wife, and so forth. To be sure, he must not expect to be *beloved* by *one* proto-friend. (184)

And it is easy to see the flaws which men of the world, on their part, would see in Coleridge. Tom Moore talks of his 'preachment.' Sam Rogers, sitting at the far end of the dinner-table, and for once not finding all heads turned in his direction, records with asperity that he 'could not make head nor tail of him.'[1] To many, he was too deficient in the human side of friendship: he often gave offence: he was accused of disloyalty. In the eye of common sense he was a bad, if only because he was a borrowing, friend. 'Friendship is a sheltering tree. . . .' On this account as much as any other, very likely, acquaintances tended to side against Coleridge when they heard of his quarrels. 'I knew before that Coleridge was a worthless friend,'[2] says Mrs. Clarkson suddenly, a propos of the Wordsworth affair.

An inability to make casual friendships is no handicap. But Coleridge was far from averse to such ac-

[1] Rogers' *Table Talk*.   [2] H.C.R., 71.

quaintanceships. He was a lonely man. Coleridge himself need never have been lonely. It was the intrusions of the unwanted third party, of S.T.C., which alienated prospective companions. However formative a relationship is likely to be, however admiring the potential disciple, such contacts are likely to be limited unless there is a certain amount of worldly finesse, a gentleness and understanding about the first approaches. Coleridge suffered from an unattractive mannerism. He suffered, as usual, from S.T.C.

The trait which most of his friends found difficult was the enormous, the appalling effusiveness with which, once they were well within his field, he assailed them. The excitement he expresses when he acquires a new friend scarcely seems as if it can be sincere. He will assure the man that he is writing a particular thought to him, and to him only. 'Burn this,' he says. But the recipient calmly files, knowing that Coleridge may easily have written the same thought, and the same admonition, to two or three others as well. Or there are embarrassing eulogies. Southey actually writes to reprimand him on this point, admitting that his dislike of them may be too intolerant, admitting that when they are true they may be excused, 'but when they are not,' he says sternly, 'there is no excuse for them.'

It might have been expected that such advice would freeze Coleridge into exaggerated impersonality, but in the very next letter he writes back:

MY DEAR SOUTHEY! the longer I live, and the more I see, know, and think, the more deeply do I seem

to know and feel your goodness; and why, at this
distance, may I not allow myself to utter forth my
whole thought by adding your *greatness*? (*L.*, 488)

No discipline of worldly tact—bitterly hurt when he had
no reason—devastatingly forgive-and-forget when no
such emotions were appropriate. He would generously
and publicly take up cudgels for friends or ex-friends
at the very moment when they were anxious to lie
low, publicly praising Southey, for instance, in the
wrong way and at the wrong time. This happened
on the occasion of Southey's attempted withdrawal
from publication of his early Jacobinical *Wat Tyler*.
'Of injudicious defenders,' writes Dorothy, 'he is the
master leader . . . He does nothing in simplicity, and
his praise is to me quite disgusting.'[1] Nothing seems to
keep down this irrepressible S.T.C., this unwanted
third party. It is an interesting demonstration of the
superiority of Coleridge to his written word as este-
ceanly adulterated that almost all these misunder-
standings started at a distance.

In youth, Coleridge had isolated himself in a
different way.

In early genius-hood, Coleridge offended by his unquestioning assumption of leadership. He annoyed
even Charles Lamb in this way. Hazlitt, after the
first feeling of hero-worship had worn off, rebelled
more and more angrily against it. 'I was, I fear, too
contemptuous with Hazlitt,' Coleridge notes in his
journal. But very soon after 1800 all this was to be

[1] K., ii. 98.

changed. S.T.C.'s reiterated cry of 'wasted talents' soon grew stronger than Coleridge's knowledge that doing is less important than being, and a spirit of what must have seemed like insincere humility takes the place of the youthful genius attitude: however obviously unrepresentative Pecksniffian traits may be they are the most difficult for generous friends to overlook.

For with the self-castigation goes an equally unattractive self-pity: not only a constant and natural description of his misery—necessary relief for him—but long medical accounts, physical symptoms, evacuatory details. To Mrs. Coleridge: You cannot have 'any adequate notion how seriously ill I am.'[1] To Wordsworth, the same. He is dying, he says: so that Wordsworth in great distress makes the long journey to London—to find him with his friends, smart and affable, holding forth to admirers at his most eloquent. And with all the self-castigation, he cannot bear castigation from any one else. 'Show me anyone made better by blunt advice,'[2] says Coleridge, sympathetic to the efforts of S.T.C. to preserve his self-respect. When S.T.C. was at his worst Coleridge was still angrily conscious of the fact that, more than any of his friends, he had the right to lead. Just because he knew his failings so well, he was never philosophical in the receiving of advice.

The species of weakness from which he suffered, is, I believe, the explanation of a puzzling side problem of Coleridge relationships—his 'monomaniac likings,'

[1] *U.L.*, i. 274.   [2] 167.

mentioned above—for Boyer, Sir John Ball, etc. These men's *characters* were superior to Coleridge's, and were strongest where his was weakest—in dependability, management of worldly affairs, mannishness. Coleridge enjoyed in them strength of character by proxy.

I receive a comfort even from my infirmities . . . in the joy of the deep feeling of the opposite virtues in the two or three whom I love. (177)

The opposite virtues he would be certain to find in headmasters and diplomatists. Esteceanism would preclude any kind of success in those professions, and would be fatal, it may be added, to editors of trenchant quarterlies. In spite of mutual animosities, there is a suspicion that Coleridge could not help a covert admiration even for Jeffrey.

But Jeffrey could not have been his friend, for two reasons which epitomise the weakness and the strength of Coleridge's associations. Jeffrey could not give the admiring sympathy weakly demanded by S.T.C., nor was he capable of the fundamental agreement in objectives, the differentiating integrity of experience, demanded by the strength of Coleridge. When Coleridge says that his instincts are dog-like, we can impatiently agree—he longs to be thrown a bone, and given a friendly kick. But it must be remembered that he says elsewhere that he means by 'dog-like,' 'with an affection upwards'; S.T.C. is, as often, caricaturing a valuable Coleridge trait. My nature needs another for support, Coleridge says, and then continues (I find this sentence after I have written the above, so well has Coleridge taught me): Another nature 'the same indeed, but dissimilar . . . the same *soul diversely incarnate.*' (164)

Again.

Coleridge on Coleridge:

There is a species of applause necessary to a poet, without which the sense of power sinks back on itself like a sigh heaved up from the tightened chest of a sick man. . . . The appreciation of good and intelligent men is my sea-breeze. (189 . . . 614)

This feeling we revere, and then there is the other, the desire for flattery.

Coleridge on S.T.C.:

Much as I *wriggle* under the burden and discomfort of the praise of people, for whose heads, hearts, and specific competence I have small respect, yet I own myself no self-subsisting mind. I know, I feel, that I am weak, apt to faint away, inwardly self-deserted. . . . (614)

Coleridge, on the contrary, could stand alone.[1] Yet it is easy to see how curious visitors, when he was older, must have seen in him the usual defensive famous veteran, whom it was obviously important not to offend, who would probably be very ready to talk, as

[1] And there is a kind of Coleridgean equivalent to this particular estecean weakness: 'In the Duck and drake projecting across the stream of Error and misery, let the Friend be as the elastic force of the water, giving a new bound to the stone and preventing its touch of the stream being the submersion.'—MS. G.H.B.

a show-piece, but who would be unlikely to listen to what was said to him. 'Exactly what I thought,' says the young visitor, who had not been without hopes, perhaps, of reforming this great man of an out-of-date generation to his own way of thinking. 'Precisely. Living on his reputation—if indeed he has ever done anything else.' Thus Emerson recalls his own visit, to Highgate, youthfully sceptical, as a failure!

> As I might have foreseen, the visit was rather a spectacle than a conversation, of no use beyond the satisfaction of my curiosity. He was old and pre-occupied, and could not bend to a new companion and think with him.

Poor Coleridge's only defence against this sort of thing was private complaints to his notebook. The young men (who invite themselves) 'put questions that cannot be answered but by a return to first principles, and then they complain of me as not conversing but lecturing.' Coleridge has to conclude that these single exhibition meetings are bound to be unreproductive, and that

> the man of genius should live as much as possible with beings that simply love him, from relationship or old association, or with those that have the same feelings with himself; but in all other company he will do well to cease to be the man of genius, and make up his mind to appear dull. . . . (193)

It is clear that friendship, for Coleridge, was neither easy nor simple. But in spite of these difficulties,

Coleridge achieved more than one famous association—formative 'proto-friendships' as he called them.

Poole, of Stowey, Coleridge always considered his first friend. Why does he leave out Southey, whom he connects with the 'fairest of all fair dreams'? With Pantisocracy and his first real youth? The reason is that in these years neither Coleridge nor Southey had reached the age when real exchange was possible. Their friendship is embryo, rather than proto. Its language is romantic: 'Coleridge and I are seated at the same table. Our names are written in the book of destiny.'[1] There was rapid disillusionment. Like most friendships formed in idealism, its collapse was hastened by each party constituting himself moral spur to the other. First there was Southey's moral attitude over C.'s backslidings from Frickerdom: it was Coleridge's turn when Southey's reception of a legacy from an aunt coincided with waverings from communism—and so, back and forth, with Southey more and more unarguably in the right, more and more insistently the adviser, more and more kindly— even ostentatiously—father to Coleridge's neglected children. As Wordsworth said (after Coleridge's death) Southey took 'too rigid a view'[2] of his friend. He never could have been the man for Coleridge. There was too much of brass in him, notoriously difficult to fuse: brass defences without, and within brass tacks of common sense to bring the discoverer up short. His moment of youth had come and gone. Coleridge,

[1] R.S., i. 231.   [2] Moore's *Reminiscences*.

note, made contact with most of his friends at the prime season of their lives.

Next came Lamb. School friendship was probably renewed when Coleridge made him the confidant of his difficulties over the Fricker engagement. For a year after his marriage they wrote each other immense letters. It is difficult to know in what direction Coleridge felt himself to be expanding with Charles Lamb, because his side of the correspondence is lost. It is certain that the early Charles was very different from the consistently attractive, picturesque character, the man of amusing and genial sapience for which the word 'Lamb' now stands. He plunged, he passed from extremes of hopefulness and resignation, he bit off more than he could chew, he wanted, above all, to be a great poet: and his hero was Coleridge. Their correspondence, according to his later confession, he regarded as the 'pride of his life.' Coleridge was his standard of excellence: he stood for the rightness and purpose of the world.

> I love to write to you. I take a pride in it. It makes me feel less meanly of myself. It makes me think myself not totally disconnected from the better part of Mankind.

He sincerely thought that *Religious Musings* was the noblest poem in the language, next after *Paradise Lost*. He sent his verses to Coleridge for criticism, and would have the joy of seeing them published in the neighbourhood of Coleridge's own lines, with slight editings, refinements in Coleridge's earlier manner, a line filled out with an 'Ah, me!' . . . 'Merlin' substituted for some less suitably romantic name, etc. Nor was Coleridge backward in living up to this part. Nevertheless, though it survived the inevitable quarrel, the friendship never progressed beyond these opening stages. There was no mutual reduction to elements, and apprehension of elemental differences.

Lamb was not good at elements. In early life his conception of fundamentals seems to have been Schillerian: later, his huge misfortunes drove him to books as a refuge from sorrow, not as a key to its meaning. Here Coleridge could have helped him: but to Lamb, Coleridge's eloquence in the realms of personality and experience seemed like 'goodness,' or religious instruction. 'I might have been a worthless character but for you,' he used to say. 'As it is, I do possess a certain improvable portion of devotional feelings.' After the family tragedy, he wrote to Coleridge asking for 'as religious a letter as possible.' Coleridge obeyed all too precisely. Your mother dead? he writes with gusto: 'It is sweet to be roused from a frightful dream by the song of birds and the gladsome rays of the morning' . . . *a fortiori* it is sweet to be awakened by the hallelujahs of angels. 'I charge you . . . come to me.' Coleridge followed this letter with another, and then a third, more religious than ever. Lamb began to murmur:

'Your letters,' he says, 'especially please us when you talk in a religious strain; not but we are offended occasionally with a certain freedom of expression,

a certain air of mysticism. . . . Let us learn to think
humbly of ourselves. . . .'

The good man was beginning to look to Lamb like
a man fond of seeming good. How was he to know
that it was all a cheeky parody of Coleridge, by S.T.C.?
Very likely Lamb felt out of it with Coleridge's new
friends, the Wordsworths. Coleridge must often have
seemed off-with-the-old-and-on-with-the-new after the
unrecapturable first year. Nor would Lamb have been
interested in the endless talk of Spinoza, and the
doctrine of necessity. Moreover, he must have felt
that he had the right to be treated with more tact
by a man so obviously successful in the realm in which
he had failed, as he felt, for ever—poetry. Lamb had
an aversion to competence; he tended to be suspicious
of the successful. His doubts grew as Coleridge's air of
de haut en bas increased, and received fearful confirma-
tion when it was repeated to him, on the eve of Coleridge's departure with the Wordsworths for the Con-
tinent, that he had said ' "Poor Lamb" (these were
his last words) "if he wants any *knowledge* he may apply
to me." '

No wonder Lamb was thunderstruck. He must have
longed to puncture the image of what he now thought
was an indefensible sacrosanctity. He must have
mocked with exquisite pertinence—('as friend Coleridge said when he was talking bawdy to Miss — —
"to the pure all things are pure," ' etc.). He was to
hero-worship no more contemporaries. But Lamb
was a bad quarreller. Moreover, Coleridge's *de haut*

en bas days were soon to be over for ever. It was not
long before he was to cease for ever to be identifiable
with 'success.' Moreover, in a few years, he gained
the general disapproval of the world, just the kind of
condition to ensure Lamb's loyal support for ever.
Lamb was not the man for Coleridge. There could
be no exchange of worlds, with Lamb cultivating an
attractive and beautiful character at the expense of
his personality. Yet the friendship was far from barren.
Lamb's description, recorded with easy precision
throughout the letters, is far the best picture of the
external Coleridge. Almost alone of Coleridge's contemporaries, also, he kept himself permanently from
judging his friend in terms of conventional morality,
or by any other irrelevant standard. He never took
the 'what a pity' attitude. He never allowed anyone
to say, 'poor Coleridge' (though Coleridge himself
indulged that patronising adjective to the end).[1] He
seemed to apprehend his friend's greatness by special
alert-genial methods of his own. He always regarded
him as a greater man than Wordsworth. And he
realised that Coleridge had to be taken more for what
he was than for what he wrote. The more I see of
Coleridge, he said 'in the quotidian undress and re-
laxation of his mind, the more cause I see to love
him, and believe him a *very good man*, and all those
foolish impressions to the contrary fly off like morning
slumbers.' It almost seemed, so quickly did it follow,
as if he mourned Coleridge's death with his own.

[1] 'Almost all the *sparkles* and *originalities* of his [Hazlitt's] Essays are,
however, echoes from poor Charles Lamb.' 666. And *cf. ante.*

But the first proto-friend, the first confidant of the mysteries, was Poole. "You were my first Friend,' Coleridge wrote later, 'in the higher sense of the word; so must you for ever be among my very dearest.' The history of the evolution of this association would be a complete description of Coleridge in the period 1796–7, years just before the advent of the Wordsworths. At first there is not much of record, judging by Coleridge standards. Very soon Poole becomes 'my beloved Poole,' and receives philosophical and sanitary intimacies: but Coleridge's deep certainty, before he went to Stowey, that he was about to grow in some way, that he needed a friend to help him, and that Poole was to be the man, is shown by his agony (in a well-known series of letters) when he imagines Poole is fighting shy of him, and putting difficulties in the way of his coming to Stowey, a panic like that of a man struggling for life. Poole was the first friend of Coleridge to be connected with an access of life.

He had all the qualifications which Coleridge needed. He showed high admiration, he showed the sympathy which Coleridge found necessary for his comfort, he had the kind of worldliness and dependability with which Coleridge liked to live, feeling the inconvenience of his own lack of these qualities mysteriously eased thereby.

Poole is one of those men who have one good quality, namely that they always do one thing at a time. . . . My mind is in general of the contrary make. (*L.*, 460)

167

Above all, there was fundamental agreement between them, as there could never have been between Coleridge and Lamb. They were interested, that is to say, in the same kind of problems, and could explore them together. There were vicissitudes, and there was one condition which Poole did not fulfil. His own physical and psychological health was so perfect that he was never able to show really patient sympathy with Coleridge's symptoms, nor with his method of allaying them.[1] Nevertheless, he was the first man to whom Coleridge could write thus:

I need not observe, my dear friend, how unutterably silly and contemptible these opinions would be if written to any other but to another self.

What precise development Poole helped to fertilise in Coleridge may be discoverable. It may have been through Poole that he first began to realise new possibilities in philosophy. He seems to have felt that in some way Poole was 'beyond' mechanist, necessitarean doctrines. There is much material here for a future study.

There is material enough, almost, for an epic, in the friendship to which Poole had to take second place[2] —that between Coleridge and the Wordsworths. William and Dorothy gave Coleridge a world which included Poole's and more. The fundamental agreement was there, the sympathy and the admiration; and the cool dependability of Wordsworth, with its

[1] *Cf.* S. ii. 117.   [2] *Cf.* S. ii. 7 ff.

greater reserve, was able to relieve Coleridge of these deficiencies in himself even more effectively than could Poole. 'How infinitely preferable Wordsworth's coolness is to Coleridge's heat,' Crabb Robinson says somewhere. Crabbomorphistic judgment—but a good description of the foundation of a well-balanced friendship. Also, there was Wordsworth's genius, his success in what Coleridge conceived to be the highest activity of man, the possibility of 'affection upwards,' of self-enlargement. Later on Coleridge found his own failure with his family made more bearable by Wordsworth's dignified success in this part of life: Coleridge even was able to be admired brother, brother-in-law, husband, father, by proxy. But this belongs to another part of the history.

The conditions, the causes, and the emergent properties of this friendship need and will one day get Homeric treatment. I suggest two contrasting elements which may seem pertinent to the main theme.

At first the relationship was the most perfect *exchange*. The mutual admiration was equally balanced. At Stowey, hardly a day passed without a meeting. Not only in writing, of the arts of communication, is there a rightness of proportion between the general and the particular. The Wordsworths—Dorothy especially—had the power to particularise, the ability to say 'Look!' Coleridge could complement this with an equally exceptional gift in saying 'Compare!' He perfectly made up the balance, with generalisations as concrete, as seminative, as the most pristine fact or example. Coleridge was to say later of the Preface to the *Lyrical Ballads*: It arose 'out of conversations so frequent that with few exceptions we could scarcely, either of us, positively say who first started a particular thought.' These conversations led to something more important than the Preface. They accelerated in Coleridge the growth of certain apprehensions. Of the nature of poetry: of the nature of genius: of the nature of experience: of the nature of knowledge. Dorothy's power to say *look*, Wordsworth's power to *be*, brought to life a new Coleridge, to whom the external and internal events of the past seemed as if they belonged to a former existence. He was two years reaping the first harvest of this friendship, before he went off to Germany to begin the completion of the knowledge which his friends had started in him.

The affectionate admiration of the Wordsworths continued, of course, after the collapse of Coleridge's health. Even after many experiences of Coleridge's exaggerated self-pity Wordsworth still wrote, in 1804, when his friend was about to leave England:

> MY DEAREST COLERIDGE, — Your letter informing me of your late attack was the severest shock to me I think I have ever received. . . . Heaven bless you for ever and ever. No words can express what I feel at this moment. Farewell, farewell, farewell.

And when Coleridge returned, in 1806, the Wordsworths were even preparing to move south, because the Lake climate did not suit him. For a year or two more, Coleridge is still 'wonderful' to Dorothy. But loyalty was beginning to be tested. The estecean traits were spreading and flourishing—not the least obviously when he was in the Wordsworth household. In spite of what Lamb called Coleridge's power of 'picking up wonderfully the next moment' ('yet how C. does rise up, as it were, from the dead':—Dorothy), the give-and-take of the friendship was over. In the early days it would have been good to hear Coleridge's anger against a lady insufficiently awe-struck in her comments on the *Leech-Gatherer*,[1] or to hear him say with innocent pride:

> It is with no feeling of idle vanity that I speak of my importance to the Wordsworths.

But now Coleridge's manly reverence had changed to a fatal feeling of inferiority; ever since his return from Malta, Coleridge had been drawing too extravagantly on the virtue with which Wordsworth could refresh him. Dependence is fatal to friendship. Reading its history, in Crabb Robinson or de Sélincourt's *Dorothy Wordsworth*, it seems strange that the quarrel did not come sooner. The Wordsworths were too generous. Coleridge, as I have suggested,[2] almost had to create the misunderstanding which enabled him to break away from their destructive kindness. Once the break had been made, reconciliation, by reason of the processes of life (and the absence of corresponding processes in Wordsworth), was impossible,[3] and Wordsworth it was who died. Coleridge was reduced to

[1] R.B.L., 125.   [2] *P.*, 69 *ante.*
[3] '. . . after fifteen years of such religious, almost superstitious idolatry and self-sacrifice. Oh, no! no! that, I fear, can never return.' (*L.*, 612)

chaos, and the gradual reassembling of the elements reconnected him with life.

The two former friends remained unsympathetic. The *Biographia* chapters on Wordsworth, in spite of the great eulogies, show fundamental aversion. After the publication, Wordsworth's coldness increased. Taken with the unconscious dyspathy, the praise seemed like whitewashing. Later, Coleridge would hint at the decline of Wordsworth's faculties.[1]

Wordsworth was able to patronise Coleridge through S.T.C.:

> No man . . . whose happiness depends on the opinions of others can possibly comprehend the best of my poems. (H.C. Rob., 49)

He had long held that Coleridge was 'finished,' and in 1830 Dorothy notes that Coleridge is publishing some new work 'on the old abstruse subjects.'[2] Gone is her memory of the Coleridge who talked to her so enchantingly of those very subjects, with such all-clarifying eloquence. His later development was completely outside their lives. Wordsworth would at times lend sympathetic attention, but now there seemed some truth in Coleridge's comment in the *Biographia*:

> the sympathy of a contemplator, rather than a fellow-sufferer or co-mate. (297)

Wordsworth was suffering from strength, as Coleridge had suffered from weakness, of character. The firmness of the external Wordsworth spread fatally, con-

---

[1] H.C. Rob., 78.   [2] H.C.R., 220.

gealing deeper and deeper to the vital centre, and qualities admirable in this external character proved fatal to his individuality. Much later, Wordsworth warmed again towards Coleridge. There was another tour to Germany even, the three together again. Near Coleridge's death, Wordsworth wrote:

He and my beloved sister are the two beings to whom my intellect is most indebted.

Coleridge died, and Wordsworth felt his death with unexpected force. He often spoke of him: and there was always his manuscript *Prelude*, and those Coleridge reminiscence lines which he must have read moved by heaven knows what complexity of feelings —lines which have since become hackneyed, but are never quite stale, recalling 'that summer, under whose indulgent skies upon smooth Quantock's airy ridge we roved . . . Thou in bewitching words with happy heart . . .' etc.

Et cetera.

O Good God! why do such good men love me!

His association with Wordsworth was the last 'affection upwards,'[1] the last outdrawing through friendship. After his recovery there was no further evolution. He was still able, however, to perfect his powers of consciousness and expression by means of receptive and sympathetic men, such as the Morgans,

[1] 'Coleridge and Thelwall,' 'Coleridge and Tom Wedgwood,' 'Coleridge and Humphry Davy' especially, would be worth separate treatment, all important associations, if subordinate to the contemporary 'Coleridge and Wordsworth.'

or Gillman, or, later younger acquaintances like J. H. Green, Allsop, Irving. These latter were disciples. The Gillmans represented the last of the 'perpetual relays which were laid along Coleridge's path in life' —men with no gifts of the kind which posterity ever hear of, but who nevertheless, by their intuitive recognition of greatness, and longing for its contact, acquire themselves an enviable honour. Gillman decided to dedicate himself to Coleridge, it seems, at their first interview, when Coleridge was neither physically nor mentally in a state likely to propitiate a stranger. Coleridge was to take up residence on the very next day. 'I looked with impatience,' wrote Gillman, 'for the morrow.' We respect the impatience, and we are jealous of its cause.

6

PLATONISTS AND
ARISTOTELIANS

... in this connection may be mentioned the poet S. T. Coleridge, whose philosophy, deeply influenced by Kant, Schelling, and the rest of the German Transcendentalists, forms a link between the idealism of the Cambridge Platonists and our nineteenth-century Hegelians.—*Any historical manual of philosophy.*

THE above quotation will do for Coleridge's place in English philosophy. I collect here some thoughts and quotations to suggest that his position is outside it.

Confusing the whole question of 'Coleridge and Philosophy' are two misconceptions which have worked their way into the popular or text-book view of Coleridge.

The first is connected with the belief that it is 'a pity that Coleridge took to metaphysics.' 'He lost himself in metaphysics.' 'His visit to Germany was the ruin of him, and meant the giving up of poetry for German metaphysics.' And so on.[1] The inference is that the

---

[1] Since this chapter was written, Mr. Richards' *Coleridge on the Imagination* has appeared, to render many of my paragraphs redundant. Several of the themes shadowily touched on here have now been dealt with more precisely and with greater authority. Mr. Richards goes much more deeply into the anatomy of 'Know Thyself,' the 'Philosophy of Feeling,' and Coleridge's expressed sense of the inadequacy of language as an instrument of thought. My opening paragraph here is a theme of

kind of metaphysics Coleridge took to were 'vaguely mystical.' Forceful contemporaries seem to have encouraged the misunderstanding. Hazlitt—Carlyle—Wordsworth. Carlyle's *passing* references to Coleridge (as opposed to the eloquent honour he does him in his principal essay) are nearly always to 'Coleridgean moonshine,' his 'prophetic or magician' character (subtle swivelling of truth), 'Coleridgean legerdemain,' 'mysticism' (spoken derogatorily). There are Coleridge's own references—*e.g.* in the *Ode*—regretting that since the departure of his poetical faculty there is nothing left for him but to 'chase metaphysical game.' The great majority of subsequent writers have been equally deprecating—*e.g.* Leslie Stephen and Dr. Mackail. Traill, in the *English Men of Letters* 'Coleridge,' regretting that Coleridge did not give up metaphysics *for politics*. Or compare J. M. Robertson:

> His faculty being one of verbal expression, he tends to make verbal exercise take the place of investigation . . . he expects to turn the tide of human thought by fixing the sense of such terms as 'reason' and 'understanding . . .'

Such a critic as Professor Lowes, infinitely sympathetic to another side of Coleridge, quotes with approval Professor Garrod's even more authoritative suggestion that there is 'not much in' the reason-understanding distinction. And where the more general critics have

Mr. Richards' first chapter. But I have made no cuts, believing that even if the cross-illumination of my own very different angle throws no extra light, my quotations will help.

spoken comparatively unfavourably, almost all philosophers have ignored the subject altogether.[1] The fallacies and question-begging behind this misconception become clear when its causes are considered. Some of these apply equally to the unpopularity of most of the rest of Coleridge's published work, and have already been suggested. Obvious are (1) Coleridge's disregard for the amenities of his readers, typified in the atrociously unattractive titles—often hortatory—which he gave to those pamphlets in which his philosophy is best expressed; aggravated by a habit of embedding his most profound intuitions within a framework of irrelevant affirmation, or in notebooks not published till long after his death; exemplified in his tendency to think aloud before listeners sometimes antipathetic to, generally ignorant of, that general drift to his meaning, those fundamental premises without the understanding of which much of what he said was meaningless.[2]

(2) There is much apparent confusion or ambiguity in Coleridge's philosophy. Paradoxically, this is a fault of his clarity. There is not in Coleridge any precise doctrine *made* clear for the sake of intelligibility. Coleridge is not explaining himself to himself. He is carrying distinctness—consciousness—a little deeper than it has been carried before, and in describing his discoveries he is at a loss sometimes whether to fabri-

[1] Those who have not (Shawcross, Muirhead, Snyder) have till lately been patronised for their efforts.
[2] *E.g.* the sentences of deep self-enquiry quoted here on p. 210 were contained in a letter *to Godwin*, who cannot conceivably be supposed to have taken the trouble even to be mystified by them.

cate new words or to give a new meaning to old ones. There is also a half-conscious distrust of the too-easily comprehensible. Incisive, periodic sentences are a barrier between the individual trying to convey unique experience and the individual anxious to receive it.

(3) On the other hand, there is some culpable confusion, which is the result of confusion in himself, between Coleridge and S.T.C. Coleridge was a daring pioneer in self-exploration, too daring for S.T.C., who would bring his master hurrying back to the safe cover of controversial argument. 'From the earliest times my mind has habituated itself to the vast.' And then another Coleridge lusted for minuter comforts, for doctrine of the kind called academic. During his period of greatest unhappiness especially, he tried to forget himself in the fervent comparison of different metaphysical theories. This pursuit has scarcely even a subject-matter connection with the great serious activity of his life—self-knowledge by means of the construction of a personal metaphysic. He thus uses philosophy in a confusingly twofold way—for self-forgetfulness and for self-attainment.

(4) One further cause of this prejudice—his philosophy is a close reflection of Coleridge's personality, and this personality is very far from resembling the picture, resolutely visualised by the world, of what a philosopher ought to be. Just as, in the world's eye, a poet is supposed to be dreamy, or ardent, so is a philosopher supposed to be reserved, esoteric and detached. Coleridge is none of these things.

But the best, the perfectly rational, explanation for this under-estimating will be found in the answer to the second misconception, the second misleading criticism which has repeated its way into every text-book, namely, that 'The value of Coleridge's meta-physic is adulterated by his habit of plagiarism from the German transcendental philosophers.'

'Coleridge's Debt to Germany' (with subsidiary Hamlet problems, dates of Schlegel lectures, jealous animadversions of de Quincey) seems, judging by the number of theses devoted to the subject, to be the major problem, so far, of Coleridge criticism. Yet so far as the charge of plagiarism or imitation is concerned, one fact seems to cancel out most of the discussion, namely, that the charge is not relevant. That for the Coleridge kind of philosopher, culpable plagiarism is impossible.

It is true that Coleridge was one of the few men of his time capable of being influenced—capable of fusing his own world with another's, and giving birth to a new world in the process. Further, he was perhaps the only man of his time capable of being influenced by the best thought of the new German philosophers. He alone had achieved a culture and an evolution which made him capable of seeing in Kant and still more in Schelling co-equals in experience. With de-light he acknowledged the fellow-thinkers.

Whether a work is the offspring of a man's own spirit, and the product of original thinking, will be discovered by those who are its sole legitimate judges, by better tests than the mere reference to dates. (*B.L.*, i. 104)[1]

Coleridge was not concerned with original thought for its own sake, because he was not that kind of philosopher: and now comes the final explanation of all this misapprehending, which is, that there are two kinds of philosopher, so widely separated as to be not even contrastable, as to have no common denominator but the name. The first type is the 'Eureka' philosopher, who, after much reading in the work of other metaphysicians, 'discovers' the theory which he likes best, takes up a position, defends it, adds a little to it perhaps (*i.e.* pushes its logical implications a step or two further), makes it a little more impervious to attack, in the modest belief that he is adding one more brick (however small) to the pyramid of truth. For this philosopher, plagiarism is not only possible, it is the necessary foundation. The second type does not believe in this steadily growing objective pyramid. Finding that reality can never be comprehended, in the sense of final circumscription implied by that word, he will try to express reality less abstractly, without attempting to explain it, in a series of direct apprehensions, acts of consciousness, connected organically, but not dialectically. And although he will be rendered more articulate by the study of philosophers whose experience is cognate with his own, the product of this conjunction, by all the laws of biology, will be different, will be new, will not be plagiarism. Coleridge, who

---

[1] *Cf.* p. 41. And see Nonesuch *Coleridge*, Index, 'Plagiarism,' for a selection of Coleridge's many references to this theme.

is of this second type, is expressive on the subject of this opposition. Choosing the terms 'Aristotelian' and 'Platonist' for the two types, and speaking as 'Platonist,' he says:

> With regard to Philosophy, there are half a dozen things, good and bad that in this country are so nicknamed, but in the only accurate sense of the term, there neither are, have been, or ever will be but two essentially different Schools of Philosophy: the Platonic, and the Aristotelian. To the latter, but with a somewhat nearer approach to the Platonic, Emanuel Kant belonged; to the former Bacon and Leibnitz and in his riper and better years Berkeley—And to this I profess myself an adherent—*nihil novum, vel inauditum audemus,* though as every man has a force of his own, without being more or less than a man, so is every true Philosopher an original, without ceasing to be an Inmate of Academies or of the Lyceum. (683)

Or

> Every man is born an Aristotelian, or a Platonist . . . They are the only two classes of men beside which it is next to impossible to conceive a third.[1]

This is the only opposition in the world of philosophy or in the world of men. A disagreement, Coleridge might say, between two 'Aristotelians'—say, Hume and Beattie—is no disagreement. There is only a difference in ability. Obviously argument between 'Plato' type and 'Aristotle' type is impossible, though Coleridge

[1] Thus Coleridge maintains that Dryden *could* not, Dante *must* have been a Platonist.

likes to record, from the point of view of 'Plato,' instances of the ease with which 'Aristotle' can be refuted. Speaking of the 'mere logician' Sir James Mackintosh, and his way of holding the floor, he says: 'If there had been a man of genius in the room, he would have settled the question in five minutes.' And he points to the ease with which Mary Woolstonecraft (perhaps scarcely 'Plato' philosophic) could turn the arguments of Godwin as an instance of the 'ascendency which people of imagination exercised over those of the mere intellect.'[1]

Coleridge's reservation of the name 'Philosopher' to transcendentalists confines boundaries:

> I say, then, that it is neither possible or necessary for all men, or for many, to be Philosophers. There is a *philosophic consciousness*, which lies beneath or (as it were) *behind* the spontaneous consciousness natural to all reflecting beings. . . .[This] is exclusively the domain of pure philosophy, which is therefore properly entitled *transcendental*, in order to discriminate it at once, both from mere reflection and *re*-presentation on the one hand, and on the other from those flights of lawless speculation which, abandoned by *all* distinct consciousness, because transgressing the bounds and purposes of our intellectual faculties, are justly condemned as transcendent. (245)

By marking and underlining one's Coleridge—an essential business of reading him—it is possible to sift

---

[1] *Hazlitt*, P. P. Howe.

out some kind of historical account of the decline in England of philosophy (in the sense thus restricted). The period from Locke to Hume, commonly regarded as a golden age of thought, Coleridge describes as 'decay.' He talks of 'the long eclipse of philosophy' and 'the transfer of that name to physical and psychological empiricism,'[1] and 'the non-existence of a learned philosophical class.' He cites the indifference to philosophy of such thought leaders as Burke and Johnson as indirect evidence of the fact that the word 'Philosopher' was connected with 'lucky Frenchified [?Condillacised] experimenters.' There are not now, Coleridge complains, even schools of thought. They say to him: 'I hear you are a Swedenborgian!' 'Would to God,' he replies fervently, 'that *they* were *anything*.'[2] The popular philosophy, which, in the eyes of Coleridge, took the place of real philosophy among his contemporaries, he was the better able to describe for having himself once been in its grip. (*Cf.* p. 32 *ante*). There are few pages[3] of his later books which have not a reference somewhere to the errors of the mechanical philosophy—mistaking 'the causes, the conditions, and the occasions of our becoming *conscious* of certain truths and realities for the truths themselves': or to the verbalism which makes it not so much philosophy as philology: above all, he derogates the mechanist's attempt to prove doctrines which are not susceptible of proof, to fix as finally right or wrong thoughts which are only true at the moment of their first utterance, as the first fruits of an experi-

[1] J.H.M., 60.   [2] 688.   [3] *Cf.* 450,, A.D.S. 128.

ence. In other intellectual realms he finds his contemporaries discussing arguments for the existence of God in which some reference to a watch seems to be the most notable element, or ethics based on the crudeness of a half-science of enlightened selfishness, elaborated by statistics. Coleridge writes it all down in his notebook, and works the extract up passionately for *Omniana*. Think of England under Alfred, he says —blood-stained, untaught. Then, gloriously, a growing, mighty empire—

> and then finally behold this mighty nation, its rulers and its wise men listening to—Paley and to—Malthus! It is mournful, mournful. (197)

The system of modern metaphysics,

> banishes us to a land of shadows, surrounds us with apparitions, and distinguishes truth from illusion only by the majority of those who dream the same dream. . . . Oh, ye that reverence yourselves, and walk humbly with the divinity in your hearts, ye are worthy of a better philosophy! Let the dead bury the dead, but do you preserve your human nature, the depth of which was never yet fathomed by a philosophy made up of notions and mere logical entities. (*B.L.*, i. 179)

Principles.

I concentrate thus, in my quotations from my marked Coleridge, on the sympathies and dyspathies of his philosophy, placing them first, because trying to understand, up to my capacity, Coleridge's starting-

point, the genus of Coleridge's thought, which must
be recognised confidently before his philosophy can
be studied at all, differing as it does from the common
stock of English philosophy, standing outside it.
Readers will supply Coleridge with blood relations,
according to their knowledge. But these will not, as
heretofore, be Schelling—will not be Kant even.
Spinoza, perhaps; Goethe, more likely. Coleridge's
starting-point is outside traditional philosophy.

Perhaps the reader, now, will suspect that the Cole-
ridgeanp rinciples and their enumeration—by processes
usually entailing a reduction to gist—belong to Coleridge
in terms of a philosophical text-book, and that they can
only be studied with understanding after full absorption of the character of the Coleridge starting-point.
But in fact the principles of Coleridge's philosophy, or
rather his way of formulating them, are most relevant
to its character. They demonstrate not gist but drift,
and the reader who does not realise this will be
confused by a seeming paradox. For as often as the
importance of allowing the direction of life to follow
its own self-differentiating course without reference
to the rules of mechanist philosophy or fixed ethical
creeds is emphasised, so often comes the word 'principles' and—almost a commandment: Live in accordance with principles. The reader will have to mark,
and compare, Coleridge's uses of this word, to find
his meaning.

First, the absolute opposition between principles
and *rules*, the rules of life which represent a plagiarised
ethic, limitations imposed on himself by the klepto-

maniac of dicta. Coleridge talks, historically, of the
'decay' of principles. The nation, he says, now judges
not by principles but by results. He mocks the tone
of voice of the man who *speaks* of principles—using
them 'as but a garnish or ornamental commonplace
in the peroration of a speech.'[1] He must have been
strong against Hume's conception of a principle, the
scientific conception, as some sort of deduction of
probability, based on the law of average. He sums up
his contemporaries by describing their actions as
grounded on the 'guess-work of general consequences'
instead of 'moral and political philosophy.'[2] But what
he means by principle—that we have to imbibe, during
the slow process of Coleridge-absorption. I quote a
more or less enlightening sentence from *The Statesman's
Manual*, where he is discussing, as often, the degradation of the word 'idea' (a decline for which Locke was
responsible) into a synonym for 'notion.'

'. . . every principle is actualized by an idea; and
every idea is living, productive, partaketh of infinity,
and (as Bacon has sublimely observed) containeth
an endless power of semination.' (*S.M.*)

The significance, for Coleridge, of 'Principles' en-
croaches on meaning called up by such words as
essential . . . central . . . productive of activity concentrated, unwasted, from the clear apprehension of its
purpose, the conscious wish directly inspired by the
unconscious will.

So Coleridge, feeling for the root of an action,

[1] 689. [2] *C.S.*, 70.

formulates its principle. Examples could be given from many sides of his activity. I think, first, of a more trivial one. He is drawing up a course of lectures (never delivered) to further the founding of London University. It will illustrate his process of principle seeking—finding a principle, from which the details may grow in definite relation. From a sketch of the Prospectus:

> ... the one true and only adequate Scheme of a University stated and unfolded from the Seed (*i.e.* the idea) to the full Tree with all its Branches. 3. ... and lastly, a plan (and sketch of the *means*) of approximating to the Ideal, adapted and applied to this Metropolis. (N.B. The Plan *in detail*, salaries only not mentioned—the particular sums, I mean.) (*A.D.S.*, 41)

This will serve as a pattern. It is in the major activities of life that Coleridge seeks to enucleate a principle.

As for law: '*Subordinate, not exclude*, as a principle for legislation, thought, the scale of life, etc.' (*L.R.*, iv. 92)

For history—'you must commence with the philosophic idea of a thing, the true nature of which you wish to find out ... an idea or self-realising theory of the constitution ... which shall comprehend within it *all* the facts which history has preserved, and shall give them a meaning as interchangeably causals or effects. ....' (508).

For art, many—*e.g.* reconciler of nature and man ... the vital and the formal must be thoroughly

187

reconciled . . . the functioning of two opposed human faculties, etc.[1]

For his æsthetic—the conception of Beauty as an Act (the reader will not know this formulation of this principle, from a MS.):[2] 'Every form of Beauty outward and objective must be contemplated as a *Product* . . . of an Intelligent Will, not wholly or principally as intelligence, but as living Will causative of reality.'

Then, above all, in two centres of Coleridge's interest does he clarify from the root upwards, by trying to enunciate the principle and to allow the workings out to take shape from it of themselves. In politics, and in the 'theory of life.'

Principle and Politics.

It happens that the significance of Coleridge's political thought has had usefully clarifying treatment from more than one source.

In at least two of these summaries it has been shown that the evolution of Coleridge's political ideas really was an evolution—not as in the case of Southey a mere tergiversation from Young Man Left to Old Man Right—and that the ideas really were ideas and not notions. Muirhead discusses Coleridge's *Church and State* (*On the Constitution of the Church and State according to the Idea of Each*). Speaking of the deadness and materialism of the politics of the Waterloo era, he says: 'Into this welter of opinions Coleridge introduced an entirely new note by calling on men to return to

[1] For the original of this epitome *v.* A.D.Sn., 29.
[2] *E.g.* 2800, f. 67.

the Idea or ultimate aim of both Church and State and reorientate themselves in the light of it on the problem of their present duties.'[1]
'Return to the idea . . . reorientate' is a summary of Coleridgean aim which describes more than his political life. In politics especially, Coleridge was careful to know motives. He underlines them, for instance, in the Prospectus of the *Watchman*. It would seem too ludicrously paradoxical, I suppose, if it were suggested that there was anything of value in the *thought* of that pamphlet, with all C.'s famous comic tales about it. Yet read in the all-qualifying context of the life and works of Coleridge—

A people are free in proportion as they form their own opinions . . . without previous illumination a change in the *forms* of Government will be of no avail. . . . We actually transfer the Sovereignty to the People, when we make them susceptible of it.

He underlines the same thought in *Biographia*:

If then unanimity grounded on moral feelings has been among the least equivocal sources of our national glory, that man deserves the esteem of his countrymen, even as patriots, who devotes his life and the utmost efforts of his intellect to the preservation and continuance of that unanimity by the disclosure and establishment of *principles*. (*B.L.*, i. 124)

And yet—remember that not one half of one per cent. of Coleridge's admirers have ever understood or wanted to understand the import of his political writings, for reasons as obvious as they are irrelevant.

[1] J.H.M., 164.

The preconception has always been that he changed, in accordance with physiological processes so familiar as to be without interest, from youthful Jacobin to arch-Tory. It is forgotten that the Jacobinism never existed, except in larval Cambridge days of pre-youth. Much more important, it is not realised that Pantisocracy has nothing whatever to do with the psychology and motives of juvenile leftishness. I do not know how far the standard monographs on Coleridge's politics agree here—but in my sketch of his evolution I presented Pantisocracy as birth struggle of the true Coleridge, Coleridge's first attempt to actualise an Idea (having at Cambridge been *actuated by* notions) —to create a mode and activity of life proper to himself. More attention is paid to Coleridge's misleading description of Pantisocratic days as the fairest of all fair *dreams* than to the less-known passage in the *Friend*, where he says so emphatically that it was to this time in his life that he owed 'much of whatever I at present possess of insight into the nature of individual Man.'[1] It is natural to regard his elderly aversion to Reform and Emancipation Bills with fatherly indulgence or filial superiority, forgetting the true Coleridgean reasons for this aversion—that the Bills were (of necessity) fostered by appeals to popular feeling, to emotions rather than to motives, to feelings of the very kind which led, through the obscuring of the true dessire of the individual, to the race-destroying factory conditions and *laisser-faire* methods against which Coleridge himself was conscientiously if ineffectively polemical.

[1] 432.

It is forgotten, for the obvious reason, the usual reason, that the estecean elements in the case are the most obvious. Estecean wish to please the conventional, and a natural desire, common to all who are too firmly gripped by their character, that external conditions should remain unchanged for its preservation.

The second subject which I cite as particularly evocative of Coleridgean principles is one which, for urgent contemporary reasons, Coleridge is likely to be more and more frequently consulted in the future. Coleridge called it the 'Theory of Life,' and it is pertinent to us because it seems that we are now for all working purposes bound by a theory of life inadequate, whether as explanation or metaphor, to the phenomena it is meant to cover. A nineteen-thirties' reference is relevant here for another reason, namely, that our own 'theory of life' is a grandchild of the mechanico-corpuscular doctrines of Coleridge's own contemporaries: and by remembering how dubious are the laws which we ourselves take for granted, we can understand how many of the principles—theories rather—of 1800 a Coleridge would find it necessary, for his own apprehension of the roots of the matter, to supersede. Our modern theory of life is some variant of evolution or progress concepts. It is a theory tallying perfectly with the demonstrated facts—fitting them so closely as to be for this very reason deeply suspect as a principle of so changing and unpredictable a thing as life. Such a criticism is easy to make. Or it is easy to point out that the only elements in nature which are demonstrable, and the only facts therefore considered necessary to account for, are the quantitative facts, and that the qualitative elements, the ebb and flow, the sudden and unpredictable uncoilings of life, are left out. What is difficult is to formulate a principle which will include these elements.

On such a subject as this[1]—so near the root of roots that to express it most tongues have to fall back on words made dignified, and trite, by ancient use—in these deep waters Coleridge is masterfully at home.

The Principle of Process.

There is no single chapter, of course, in which Coleridge summarises his views. But he writes more than once closely and even polemically to this point, to this subject of the life principle.

He does not like the contemporary life theories:

> I attach neither belief nor respect to the Theory, which supposes the human Race to have been gradually perfecting itself from the darkest Savagery, or still more boldly tracing us back to the bestial as to our Larva, contemplates Man as the last metamorphosis, the gay *Image*, of some lucky species of Ape or Baboon. (469)

As an image of life, he believes the 'Ourang-Outang theory of the origin of the human race' a poor substitute for the first ten chapters of Genesis.[2]

---

[1] *Cf.* Coleridge's important philosophical letter, No. 285 of *U.L.*, on the need for a metaphysic of quality.

[2] *C.S.*, 67 ff.

Of contemporary pictures of life, he prefers the 'scale of beings' of which Pope and Johnson talked, a metaphor to which his own analogy bears a superficial resemblance: but Coleridge brings the image to life—makes it a metaphor of *life*. In *Aids to Reflection*, and *Hints Towards the Formation of a More Comprehensive Theory of Life*, he draws the scale of being from the elements to the more complex materials, and then (with inference that the distinction between 'organic' and 'inorganic' is artificial) to the lowest forms of 'life,' describing a new isolation of differentiation in each successive form, a unity in the individual embracing a wider complexity, a tendency, in the 'higher' forms, to an ever-increasing integrity of individuation. 'Specialisation' is our word, but it is very far from being a synonym. 'Increase of specialisation,' with its utilitarian emphasis, is equally applicable to the evolution of machines. A 'principle of individuation' is not.

Coleridge's metaphor for the appearance of man in the scale belongs to another context. 'In man,' he says, 'the individuality is not only perfected in its corporeal sense, but begins a new series beyond the appropriate limits of physiology.'[1] The name Coleridge gives to this new kind of intensity is 'soul.' On the phrase 'And man became a living soul' he comments:

> He did not merely *possess* it, he *became* it. It was his proper *being*, his truest *self*, *the* man *in* the man. (450)

[1] 469.

In this sentence we are near to the principle of principles, to Coleridge's principle of life. 'He *became* it.' Coleridge, like Goethe, regards the difference between life and death as the difference between the becoming and the become. In Coleridge's own borrowed phrase—between the *natura naturans* and the *natura naturata*. If we could absorb Coleridge into our culture we would find that for our everyday philosophy of progress would be substituted a philosophy of process, with aim of enquiry not 'what next stage' but 'what becoming?' In each species of life, Coleridge writes, the 'conditions of its *existence* are to be sought for in that which is *below* it; the grounds of its *intelligibility* in that which is *above* it.'[1] A sentence wonderfully descriptive of the element which we sometimes try to cover by the inadequate word 'advance.' We realise that the 'flow' of life is not the flow of a stream.

A being that existed for itself only in moments each infinitely small and yet absolutely divided from the preceding and following, would not exist for itself at all. (*C.S.*, 194)

*

Nature is able to reconcile chasm with continuity, to vault and nevertheless to glide. (J.H.M., 121)

*

Isolated perceptions, to be worked up, if Coleridge had not been Coleridge, into an already half-projected science in terms of life.

Coleridge, seeing the life principle in all things, is

[1] 466.

receiving from the world what he gives. For him, not only a bird, young child, or flower is obviously alive, but just as much a rock, a cloud, a word, a principle, a book, has life also. 'It is necessary, for working purposes only, to regard earth, air, and water as dead.'[1] *Whatever is, lives*, he says. Which, interpreted, means that Coleridge lives, throughout every level of his activity and consciousness. So it follows, what must often be repeated, that Coleridge is both possessed of life and conscious of it. 'All men,' he says, 'live in the power of Ideas which work in them, though few live in their light.'[2] He is one of the very few.

A Coleridge Commandment.

Principles, though not of the Coleridge kind, are sometimes found in the neighbourhood of an ethic: of *thou musts*, and *thou must nots*.

And no doubt from the Coleridge philosophy an ethic could be constructed, even rules of life, although the extensive alterations in a man which the absorption of Coleridge will bring about are not of the kind which depend on obedience to commandments.

From my own Coleridge reading there is one commandment which I remember that he emphasises: it is

Thou must think.

The characteristic of this age, Coleridge says, is the number of 'public souls,' the 'general readiness to contribute to the public good, in science and in religion, in patriotism and in philanthropy.'[3] What

[1] 198.   [2] J.H.M., 99.   [3] 455.

is lacking now is 'the habit of referring actions and opinions to fixed laws; convictions rooted in principles; thought, insight, system. . . .

We want *thinking* Souls, we *want them.*'

'Thinking,' observe, is here removed as far as possible from 'ratiocination.' Modern thought, heaven knows how deeply in the indirect debt of Coleridge, seems to stress the importance of the unconscious. Whether scientific or *über* scientific, the unconscious seems foregrounded—either because we are removing from it what has slipped there by accident; or because we are visiting it as a tourist the tombs of a dead race, to gaze in awe. Yet what Coleridge emphasises is not the mighty extent of the *unconscious*, but (it seems the same, yet is not) the mighty possibilities of new *consciousness*. Preferring, as usual, to infuse new meaning into old words, he maintains the need for 'reflection': and the book which alone of Coleridge's works bears in its subject-matter some relation to its title is his *Aids to Reflection.* The faculty of Reflection, Coleridge says, is man's peculiar differentiation, his individuation beyond physiology.

This *seeing* light, this *enlightening* eye is Reflection . . . and all thought is but unthinking that does not flow out of this, or tend towards it. (450)

Of the subjects on which Coleridge himself most commonly reflects, Thought comes first. His famous parentheses, which break up the periods of so many pages of his prose, are generally a stepping aside to answer a sudden question . . . *why* have his thoughts taken a certain turn? And then there will be a further parenthesis to consider why he thus broke off. In thinking he prefers the longest way round, and the savouring of the various stages:

> In all processes of the understanding the shortest way will be discovered the last; and this, perhaps, while it constitutes the great advantage of having a teacher to put us on the shortest road at the first, yet sometimes occasions a difficulty in the comprehension, inasmuch as the longest way is more near to the existing state of the mind, nearer to what if left to myself, on starting the thought, I should have thought next. The shortest way gives me the *knowledge* best, but the longest makes me more *knowing*. (*A.P.*, 173)

Coleridge distinguishes two kinds of thought, that connected with notions, which are capable of being handed down from mind to mind intact, and that connected with ideas, which are never intact, which are new for each individual mind, which are seminative in the minds of others. There is now, says Coleridge, no thought of this latter kind.

We want, he says, not circulating-library-fed souls, but thinking souls. Not those who take up a book for amusement. ('Well! but in their *studious* hours, when their bow is bent, when they are *apud Musas*?')[1] We do not, he says, even want public souls: we want thinking souls.

[1] 459

The Handicap of Language.

Seeking for a cause of this deficiency, Coleridge concentrates his enquiry on the verbal element in thought. (In dealing with Coleridge, the supremely word-conscious man, the epithet must be not 'merely' verbal, but 'actually' verbal.) Language, he says, is not the ideal medium.

> I believe that processes of thought might be carried on independent and apart from spoken or written language. I do not in the least doubt, that if language had been denied or withheld from man, or that he had not discovered and improved that mode of intercommunication, thought, as thought, would have been a process more simple, more easy, and more perfect than the present, and would both have included and evolved other and better means for its own manifestations, than any that exist now. (475)

Abuses of language are to be found:

In the wing-clipping of abstract thought involved in the association of its metaphors with the concrete images from which they originally derive:

> In disciplining the mind one of the first rules should be, to lose no opportunity of tracing words to their origin; one good consequence of which will be, that he will be able to use the *language* of sight without being enslaved by its affections. He will at least secure himself from the delusive notion, that what is not *imageable*, is likewise not *conceivable*. To emancipate the mind from the despotism of the eye is a first step towards its emancipation from

the influences and intrusions of the senses, sensations and passions generally. Thus most effectually is the power of abstracting to be called forth, strengthened and familiarised. . . . (A.D.S., 127)

In the weakness of philosophers, who, content to impregnate the popular mind with only a half-approximation of the truth they want to express, will use incompletely expressive words. In time, these half-truths stagnate into non-meaning, becoming transmitters of ignorance.

In the fact that even if a truth is completely embodied in words, the words, by much repetition, will die, so that they 'will lose all the power of truth, and lie bed-ridden in the dormitory of the soul, side by side with the most despised and exploded errors.'[1]

In the fact that ' the root of the evil is *a public*,' so that now a truth, even at the time of its adequate formulation, 'conveys dangerous falsehood to ninety-nine out of a hundred.' In the end we shall have to come round 'to the *esoteric* doctrine of the ancients.'[2]

Coleridge very often emphasises this necessity of 'rescuing the stalest truths from the impotence caused by their universal admission,'[3] and himself often acts on this necessity—*e.g.* as has been shown, rescuing so pregnant a word as 'idea' from Locke's debasement of it into 'notion' (or Hume's into 'decaying impression'). The great Coleridge word 'imagination' also is a revitalisation—in Hartley it makes one short entry only, in one short paragraph (devoted to dreams).

[1] 449.   [2] 668.   [3] 174.

But the chief danger, Coleridge seems to say, greater even than the dead use of dead words, lies in too great precision of terms. Widely sundered quotations must be drawn together to illustrate this. Reduced to a formula, they seem to mean that ideas cannot best be comprehended through terms allowing too narrow a margin for personal qualification or re-creation: nor should they be expressed, except in very distant analogy, by concrete images:

> Ideas and Conceptions are utterly disparate, and Ideas and Images are the negatives of each other. (J.H.M. 97).

Coleridge believes that to give a word absolute meaning is to finish the life of that word. Coleridge would have words subject to the same law of process to which life is subject, capable of successive interpretations by successive users. He wonders much

> whether or no too great definiteness of terms in any language may not consume too much of the vital and idea-creating force in distinct, clear, full-made images, and so prevent originality. (A.D.Sn.)

And he thinks the danger lies in the attempt to confine within bounds uncircumscribable realities.

> What, then, can be the remedy for mental restlessness and lack of clarity in life but the habituation of the intellect to clear, distinct, and adequate conceptions concerning all things that are the possible objects of clear conception, and thus to reserve the deep feelings which belong, as by a natural right,

to those obscure ideas that are necessary to the moral perfection of the human being, notwithstanding, yea, even in consequence, of their obscurity—to reserve these feelings, I repeat, for objects, which their very sublimity renders indefinite, no less than their indefiniteness renders them sublime: namely, to the ideas of being, form, life, the reason, the law of conscience, freedom, immortality, God! (439)

This pinning down, this obscuring for the sake of verbal clarity, this pseudo-thought, Coleridge regards as the work of his enemy, the mechanic philosophy, 'which cheats itself by mistaking clear images for distinct conceptions, and which idly demands conceptions where intuitions alone are possible or adequate to the majesty of the Truth.'[1]

It is against the background of this kind of context that we begin to see more clearly some part of the meaning in Coleridge's phrase:

Deep thinking is attainable only by a man of deep feeling. (590)

Thou must think . . . but not in the same line, not with the same faculty, that leads to 'philosophical' musings, logical pattern making, or chain reasoning.

I almost think that ideas *never* recall ideas, as far as they are ideas, any more than leaves in a forest create each other's motion. The breeze it is that runs through them. (428)

The philosophy of . . .?
And what is this breeze? 'More precision,' his

[1] 661.

materialist opponents would have said. 'Define.'
Grant it principles, grant it a strange kind of creed,
yet still the Coleridge philosophy has no name.
What Coleridge says of thinking must come into its
description. Keats, who would have understood
Coleridge so well if he could ever have penetrated
beyond S.T.C., mentions this as one of Coleridge's
topics during their famous Highgate walk. 'Smoking
the second consciousness' is Keats' irreverent name for
the fearful and audacious process. The Philosophy of
the Second Consciousness?

This process implies an object—self-knowledge.
Coleridge's is certainly and above all things a 'Know
Thyself' philosophy:

> Believe me, Southey! a metaphysical solution,
> that does not instantly *tell* you something in the
> heart, is grievously to be suspected as apocryphal.
> (428)

To adapt a favourite word of its author, the
philosophy might have been called the Science of
Self-enucleation.

> The more consciousness in our thoughts and words
> and the less in our impulses and general actions, the
> better and more healthful the state both of head and
> heart. (*A.R.*)

A perfect distinction between the productive and
unproductive kinds of self-consciousness. 'Truth is
self-restoration.'

Since philosophy is self-discovery, each individual philosophy—and all Coleridgean philosophies must be individual—is a reflection of its creator:

> . . . we receive but what we give
> And in our life alone does Nature live.

Beyond this, there is only the 'inanimate cold world allowed to the poor loveless, ever-anxious crowd.'

> Ah! from the soul itself must issue forth
> A light . . .

The Philosophy of Feeling.

That 'Ah' is so obviously and completely against the grain not only of the philosophical temper of Coleridge's contemporaries, but of the total attitude of all English philosophy; Coleridge's divine identification is so contradictory to the more orthodox if less divine detachment, that it is no wonder he felt it necessary to disassociate himself so specifically from the Philosophy which is self-separated from life. Coleridge cannot have found it such an admirably fascinating enigma, that Hume should confess that his doubts vanished as soon as he left his study for the streets. Hume, he would have said, was continually being put out of face by his own conclusions. (*Cf.* his comment on a Humian argument: 'That there is a sophism here, every one must feel in the very fact of being *nonpluss'd* without being convinced.')[1] The Coleridgean philosophy is related to life with every degree of directness. The meanings of thought, action, and feeling

[1] *L.R.*, IV. 280.

become interfused. Perhaps Philosophy of Life—or, less nebulous, Philosophy of Feeling. It is Humphry Davy's phrase. His friend was to be, he said, the first historian of the Philosophy of Feeling.[1]

Coleridge is connected with the word in so many of its meanings. He possessed himself, to a high degree, that familiar attribute of the well-integrated man, strength of feeling. Sensitiveness, not manifested by diffident withdrawal, the result of poverty of sensation, but by strong and uncontrollable response. I am not talking of the awful exaggeration of Coleridge's 'feelings' in another sense—in reaction to what for normal people is nothing more than an evil turn of fortune, to be borne with some kind of stoicism. Though it was when his health was sound that Mrs. Coleridge was afraid to write to tell him of the death of Berkeley, for fear of the effects of the news, and though Coleridge more than once describes how he was sometimes forced, in his youth, to run away from the intensity of his own sensations, yet there are certainly opium disorganisations, estecean products, mixed with Coleridge's behaviour; for instance, in Malta when he hears of the death of John Wordsworth.[2]

[1] J.D.

[2] *P.S.*—On being abruptly told by Lady Ball of John Wordsworth's fate, I attempted to stagger out of the room (the great saloon of the Palace, with fifty people present), and before I could reach the door fell down on the ground in a convulsive hysteric fit. I was confined to my room for a fortnight after; and now I am afraid to open a letter, and I never dare ask a question of any new-comer. The night before last I was much affected by the sudden entrance of poor Reynell (our inmate at Stowey); more of him in my next. May God Almighty bless you and —— (Signed with seal, $E\Sigma TH\Sigma E$) *L.*, 497.

PLATONISTS AND ARISTOTELIANS

I am talking now of the kind of feelings which can best be described by Coleridge himself, with the definition of which the word 'pure' must be connected— 'pure' response to some external event, a direct response swamping those buffer associative ideas with which more ordinary people surround themselves for protection.

> I seem to exist . . . almost wholly within myself . . . in a particular warmth felt *all* over me . . . and am connected with *things without* me by a pleasurable sense of their immediate Beauty or Loveliness, and not at all by my knowledge of their average value in the minds of people in general. (597)

'Feelings' may be a misleading word. What Coleridge is describing has nothing to do with the immediacy of mere sensation. 'Incorporation' would be better:

> Nothing affects me much at the moment it happens. It either stupefies me, and I, perhaps, look at a merry-make and dance-the-hay of flies, or listen entirely to the loud click of the great clock, or I am simply indifferent, not without some sense of philosophical self-complacency. For a thing at the moment is but a thing of the moment; it must be taken up into the mind, diffuse itself through the whole multitude of shapes and thoughts, not one of which it leaves untinged, between [not one of] which and it some new thought is not engendered. Now this is a work of time, but the body feels it quicker with me.

One of the qualities in this personal metaphysic is the existence of feelings as a reference, as a criterion. He not only observes on them:

> Lovers in their finite state incapable of fathoming the intensity of their feelings, *help* the thought *out* by extension, commute as it were—and thus think the passion as wide in *Time* as it is deep in essence.[1]

He criticises in terms of them, and when we know Coleridge we know how full is his meaning when he refers to the 'dislocation of feeling' in the mad scene in *Lear*.

He inveighs against a narrowed significance of the word Feelings in the eighteenth century ('the feelings' sentimentally used for the emotions connected with the affairs of 'The Heart'). When he is in a cool mood towards Wordsworth he complains of the lack of this vital ingredient in Wordsworth's sympathies, which are those of a 'contemplator, rather than a fellow-sufferer or co-mate (spectator, *haud particeps*).'[2]

He warns against the wrong use of feelings, the not translating them into action, the feelings which turn inward, and the festering thoughts which imprisoned feelings bring:

> The *thinking* disease is that in which the feelings, instead of embodying themselves in *acts*, ascend and become materials of general reasoning and intellectual pride . . . viz., *feelings* made the subjects and

[1] A marginal note to Fichte's *Versuch einer Kritik aller Offenbarung*, quoted *B.L.*, ii. 292.

[2] 297.

tangible substance of thought, instead of actions, realizations, *things done*, and as such externalized and remembered. On such meagre diet as feelings, evaporated embryos in their progress to *birth*, no moral being ever becomes healthy. (184)

Fear the standing water. *Act* from feelings, Coleridge says—and the equally important corollary, Act from *feelings*, not from beliefs:

I do not wish you to act from those truths. No! still and always act from your feelings; but only meditate often on these truths, that sometime or other they may become your feelings. (159)

Coleridge can construct a philosophy of feeling because he possesses what he calls in some one else (Coleridgeomorphising) 'the very rare occurrence of strong and deep Feeling in conjunction with free power and vivacity in the expression of it.' Feelings to him are nothing unless they are conscious. 'I will cross-examine myself' on this point, he says in his notes—and words to this effect are repeated frequently.

But remember the all-qualifying context of Coleridge. Remember that he does not mean introspection. 'All sensibility is a self-finding'[1]—that gives the clue. Through his feelings he is able to develop consciousness—thus is he able to express feeling in action, the act of self-comprehension. 'Philosophy of feeling' is almost an adequate description, embracing as it does the First Commandment, Thou Must Think. In the process of Coleridge reading the distinction between

[1] *C.S.*, 193.

thought and feeling has become obscure. 'Feeling and thought must be one.' 'Feeling and act must be one.'

I feel strongly and I think strongly, but I seldom feel without thinking or think without feeling. (*L.*, 197)

*

Deep thinking is attainable only by a man of deep feeling. (590)

Of Reason.

Thought, with Coleridge, is a self-creating act—not a self-limitation by explanation or proof. Understand that, and it is possible to understand Coleridge's name for the faculty in which thought and feeling are united —Reason, the faculty by means of which those raids which knowledge makes on the seemingly unknowable are made possible.

'Philosophy of Reason' might be one of the titles we are seeking, were it not for the exclusively technical meaning which Coleridge gives to the word, surely the most ill-chosen, with most estecean disregard for the offended efforts of his readers. In a MS.[1] he refers to a 'beautiful Piece of Reasoning'—'not beautiful because it is understood as true; but because it is felt, as a [? Product] of Reason, *i.e. immediate*, and with the facility analogous to Life.' How *of Reason*? For in Coleridge's near contemporary, Hume, is not reason 'nothing but a wonderful and unintelligible instinct in our souls'? In Coleridge, the word bears none of

[1] Eg. 2800, f. 67.

the Age of Reason meanings. In Coleridge, Reason is the 'Source and Substance of Truths without Sense'; is not connected with things, but with the relations between things; is the sole faculty by which principles are made known to us. 'After all, nothing but . . .' says Hume. 'Is no less than,' says Coleridge. A difference between 'Aristotelian' and 'Platonist' is here summarised.

It is through Coleridge's definition of Reason that we understand how his purpose in life and philosophy and in religion is the same. The attempt to drown, by self-knowledge, the surface desires in the stream of the larger Will, apprehended by 'Reason.' The attempt to remove the estecean impediments by merging them in 'Coleridge,' in the stream of his own becoming.

O what is sadder than that the *crambe bis cocta* of the understanding should be and remain a foreign dish to the efficient *will*. (172)

*

Whenever by self-subjection . . . the will of the individual, the *particular* will, has become a will of reason, the man is regenerate. (*L.*, 156)

*

The first philosopher was he that first sought to *know* in order to *be*. (186)

*

My opinion is . . . that all truth is a species of revelation.

*

Revelation? The Philosophy of Revelation?

*

If there be anything yet undreamed of in our philosophy; if it be, or if it be possible, that thought can impel Thought out of the visual limit of a man's own skull and heart; if the clusters of ideas, which contribute our identity, do ever connect and unite with a greater whole; if feelings could ever propagate themselves without the servile ministrations of undulating air or reflected light. . . . (585)

If possible for any man, most possible for Coleridge.

'*My System.*'

Is this suggested philosophy in new terms, made up of new components, Coleridge's 'system'? The phrase, 'my system,' which crops up from time to time in his letters, seems strangely inadequate to all these wonders: it usually produces a mental smile in the reader.

An understandable smile, because the system part of Coleridge's philosophy has many estecean traits, features which it would be useful to earmark clearly, in order that, being recognised for what they are, they may be respectfully passed with a sympathetic salute to the human weakness. It would be soon found, for instance, that Coleridge *wanted* to perfect a system. He wanted the dignity of it. It was part of his desire for recognition. We find him earnestly debating with himself, in manuscript, whether the system shall be called 'Estēcean' or 'Estecēan.'[1] He seemed to like the

---

[1] A.D.S.

sense of safety which the very terms of his system gave him—the psychopathic desire for the ring-fence, it will be said. He liked to recite the cumbrous terms of it, as if finding pleasure in their unapproachability: Logos Propaideuticos . . . Logos Architectonicus . . . Pentad of Operative Christianity. He enjoins Poole to secrecy, as if he were plotting to overset a dynasty, when he writes to tell him that he has '*completely extricated the notions of time and space*'[1] and is going no more in future books to 'relate little adventures of himself to *amuse* people.' He convinces himself of the fact that he has a system completed—asserting sometimes that it is 'in the press,' or that the last two-thirds of *Aids to Reflection* form a complete system, or maintaining that 'no one can say I have disclosed my sentiments only in flashes and fragments. . . .'[2] He would like to make a mission of his system, make a polemic out of it even, to counteract the forces of Paleyans and mechanic philosophers. And it is in these passages, and when he is being most systematic—as in the ten Theses of the twelfth chapter of *Biographia Literaria*—that he is at his least seminative, and least fruitfully under the influence of German originals.

But whatever S.T.C. may have hankered after, Coleridge knew well where his true value as a philosopher lay. Coleridge knew that his system, if he had one, was the last step, not the first in the pursuit of knowledge. 'My illustrations swallow up my thesis,'[3] he says. This is true of the best part of his philosophical writing. He knows that he is not concerned with con-

[1] 588.   [2] *U.L.*, ii. 345.   [3] 174.

futing and belittling any more than he is with strained and difficult 'advances' in metaphysics.

What is it that I employ my metaphysics on? To perplex our clearest notions and living moral instincts? To extinguish the light of love and of conscience, to put out the life of arbitrement, to make myself and others *worthless, soulless, Godless*? No, to expose the folly and the legerdemain of those who have thus abused the blessed origin of language, to support all old and venerable truths, to support, to kindle, to project, to make the reason spread light over our feelings, to make our feelings diffuse vital warmth through our reason. (163)

Coleridge knows, and wants to emphasise that he does not, in what he says, seek to alter, to reform, or to prophesy except as the true mystic prophesies, by knowing the present. 'Demosius,' in the dialogue printed at the end of *Church and State*, has been sneering at 'Mystes':

I would get thee [as a mystic] shipped off under the Alien Act, as a *non ens*, or pre-existent of the other world to come.

MYSTES: I disagree with *pre* and *to come*. The world in which I exist [then follows a pretty analogy from the astronomer Halley, about a magnetic globe within our own] is a neat little world where light exists as on the third day of creation, before it was polarized into outward and inward . . . (*C.S.*, 184 ff.)

The great gift of Coleridge is to reconcile outward and inward, to do away, in the creation of new and vitalising distinctions, with the man-made division between subject and object.

These distinctions, and the world of thought and feeling in which they are valid, seem more important than the Coleridge system. It misses truth by the widest possible margin to say (as a critic quoted at the beginning of this chapter said) that these famous distinctions of his are verbal merely. Distinctions are outstanding in most philosophies, especially those of the eighteenth century. The power of the Coleridgean oppositions is that before them the old distinctions lose their validity—cease to be distinctions, often. It has just been shown how Coleridge transcends the distinction between thought and feeling (his reflection-and-contemplation opposition goes to a forking root of divergence so far beneath them). Instead of a Pauline Body *versus* Spirit, or a necessitarean prescience *versus* freewill, there is Fancy and Imagination, and the more mature Understanding *versus* Reason—reason not opposed, as elsewhere in the eighteenth century, to imagination, but an enlargement of it. The old distinctions seem in this context to be not more than the product of the 'understanding' only—rational interpretations of an opposition between the rational and the super·rational. Coleridge chooses the margin of an obscure book in which to write this thought:

Now prescience and freewill are in fact nothing more than the two contradictory positions by which the human understanding struggles to express successively the idea of eternity. Not eternity in the negative sense as the mere absence of succession, much less eternity in the senseless sense of an infinite time; but eternity—the Eternal; as Deity, as God. (*L.R.*, iv. 394)

The weakness of the scholastic commentators, he says, is 'excessive anxiety in the detection and display of distinctions almost always just and subtle, but too often unfruitful.'[1] Coleridge's distinctions are fruitful because they are a reassessment in terms of the only valid criterion—dead or living, become or becoming.

Among such perilous essentials talk of 'my system' has a tinge of bathos. But it may be that here, too, I am guilty of the invariable habit of Coleridge critics— wishing him to be something he is not. Coleridge perhaps was able to have a system—because he had been able to experience. It certainly has value as a unique pattern of thought. 'My system,' he says, is 'to make history scientific and science historical—to take from history its accidentality and from science its fatalism.'[2] He applies to it, in fact, the life principle. And when it is said of Coleridge[3] that he couldn't speak without showing that his thought had some part in a planetary system—this well describes, not a man who is constructing a ring fence, but one who is completing the ring of consciousness, who knows that phenomena 'refer' in the Whitman sense. With Coleridge, the desire to fix things in a system was a weakness; but the fact that in his judgment and

[1] By Turnbull. [2] A.D.S., 114. [3] *L.*, 195.

apprehensions there is a potential inter-relatedness—
this is most different. He may never have been able to
achieve the final self-sufficiency, and say, with Goethe:
'Do not, I beg you, look for anything behind phenomena. They are themselves their own lesson.' He
was not great enough (just as he certainly was not
Wildeanly small enough) to say 'Art for the sake of
Art,' 'Life for the sake of Life.' It is the limitation, or at
any rate the peculiarity, of Coleridge that he saw the
whole better than the many, except perhaps during
his two years of happiness at Stowey. Yet with his
unequalled power of knowing the relations between
things he seemed to reveal almost as much. His
generalisations have as much shock of revealing tangi-
bility about them as even a poet's particularities, the
power of his *imagination* unifying, as it seemed to him,
Coleridgeomorphising, that Wordsworth's did:

'with its streaming face unifying all at one moment
like that of the setting sun when through an inter-
space of blue sky no larger than itself, it emerges
from the cloud to sink behind the mountain.' (660)

The system, if it is a system, is not the kind to agree
or disagree with. You cannot be sceptical about it, as
Coleridge himself says.[1] You cannot even be judicial,
Coleridge's not being the kind of philosophy 'which
calls the want of imagination judgment and the never
being moved to rapture philosophy.'[2] I shall consider
myself rewarded, its creator says, if I enable men to

[1] 519.   [2] 532.

'consider what they *are* instead of *merely* what they do; so that the fig-tree may bring forth its own fruit after its own living Principle, and not have the figs tied on to its barren sprays by the hand of outward Prudence and Respect of Character.'[1]

[1] 626.

7

UNITY AND UNITARIANISM

Singular Old Rubrics

'COLERIDGE and Religion' has come to stand for the strangest and the most notorious of all the Coleridge paradoxes. This brave adventurer in self-completion, most courageous in the most difficult kind of pioneering, to whose name attaches the awe called forth by the new individual—this hero of a-morality, *tried to keep on the windy side of orthodoxy.* He tried to fit a profound philosophy with the superficialities of the religiose; dynamic principles which were to supersede the static rules of life are found dovetailed among the dogmas and pious exhortations of orthodox Christianity.

Carlyle gives persuasive, picturesque expression to this:

He . . . knew the sublime secret of believing by 'the reason' what 'the understanding' had been obliged to fling out as incredible; and could still, after Hume and Voltaire had done their best and worst with him, profess himself an orthodox Christian, and say and print to the Church of England, with its singular old rubrics and surplices at Allhallowtide, *Esto perpetua.*

This charge,[1] so confident and yet unaggressive, so humorous, seems invulnerable, and indeed remains invulnerable after full underlinings of the danger of such an over-simplification of Coleridge's evolution, after full complaints against so perverse a misunderstanding of the meaning Coleridge gave to the word 'reason,' a misunderstanding particularly culpable in Carlyle, who so perfectly comprehended such matters when Goethe spoke them, who could discourse so eloquently, for instance, on Goethe's synonym for this very word—'*Vernunft.*'

Human nature hounds, finding themselves endeared to Coleridge by his weaknesses, may smile broadmindedly; but many are turned against Coleridge for ever by their discovery of this duplicity. They are dismayed by finding out that a writer capable of feeling and knowing as deeply as Coleridge can take serious part in minor religious controversies, indulging comfortable beliefs, bargaining for post-mortem forgiveness. The man who personifies for them the intellectual freedom of the Renaissance speaks:

> You will observe, that there is no mention of rain previously to the Deluge. Hence it may be inferred, that the rainbow was exhibited for the first time after God's covenant with Noah. However, I only suggest this. (483)

[1] In a less well-known passage, Carlyle says the same thing more simply, suggesting that the obscurity of Coleridge's religious pamphlets 'arises from his anxiety to avoid the difficulties and absurdities of the common view, and his panic terror of saying anything that bishops and good people would disapprove' . . . he paid the heavy price of his own . . . 'candour and simplicity, in the hope of gaining the favour of persons like Lady —.'

Their pioneer psychologist speaks:

A question. Is there a Devil ('does he have personal self-subsistence')? Or alternatively, do there exist, a race of persons,

> so eminently wicked, or wicked and mischievous in so peculiar a kind, as to constitute a distinct *genus* of being under the name of devils?
>
> Is this second *hypothesis* compatible with the acts and functions attributed to the Devil in Scripture? O! to have had these three questions put by Melancthon to Luther, and to have heard his reply. (*L.R.*, iv. 26)

The evaluator, for them, of Christianity according to its significance in terms of modern interpretation, dispearls:

> By the bye, the fact that Christianity in any genuine or ennobling form exists only in the Northern, or rather in the temperate climates, and degenerates in proportion to the increase of Heat— say from the 40 Deg. of N.L. to the Equator—is one of deep interest for a reflecting mind. (701)

And can it be their religious leader who says:

> It is well for me that my faith in the Trinity is already well grounded by the Scriptures, and by Bishop Bull. . . . (*L.R.*, iv. 307)

How, they wonder, can Coleridge do it? They observe that he spends lonely hours writing comments in the margin of theological pamphlets, polemical *pro* or *con* some minute question of the Athanasian Creed, and all they ask is that he shall at any rate add some proviso of the 'he that hath ears to hear' order—some specific disassociation from mere orthodoxy. But instead Coleridge bewilders with:

> The object of the third volume of my 'Friend' [is to show] that religion is not revealed unless the sacred books containing it are interpreted in the obvious and literal sense of the word, and that, thus interpreted, the doctrines of the Bible are in strict harmony with the Liturgy and Articles of our Established Church. (*L.* 676)

The Bible, science of life in terms of life, in harmony with the Liturgy?

And why, in so much of his writing, the gesture of the professional preacher (*cf.* Lamb's epigram). Why would he 'raise his hands and his head in the manner which Charles Matthews so cleverly caricatured, to assert that 'Shakespeare was a man of too pure a mind to be able to depict a really worthless character'?[1] Why, in his criticism, is he more prejudiced against irreligion than against bigotry? And then why, to come down to more personal detail, does he, in later life especially, go about dressed in parson's black? Why the pious ejaculations in letters? Why the capitalisations of religious words, and a reverent tone of voice somehow adulterating the awe which is native to his subject?

Certain excuses can be made. There is the in-

[1] A.G.L.

tellectual atmosphere, especially the theological atmosphere, of his time. Quite majestic intellects were similarly engaged. Priestley, not a mean head, holding that Nelson's Victories were predicted in the 19th chapter of Isaiah: Hartley demonstrating that W:F::L or W=F2/L when W represents the love of the world; F, the fear, and L the Love of God.[1] Such superstitions, and such rationalisations of the supernatural; such an age, which found inspiration in Blair, and looked at Paley's watch to discover God, had to be fought, perhaps, with its own weapons. It might be held that Coleridge only wrote thus when he was attacking contemporary theologians, just as it is certainly true to say that he is much more orthodox when he is writing to clergymen, especially if they are also relations, as they generally were. How the Coleridge family has always run to theology the poet's great-grandson, the Rev. G. H. B. Coleridge, will regretfully tell you.

A second excusing suggestion might be, perhaps, that Coleridge purposely wrote esoterically and exoterically in the same book.

There are, he writes, times when the few who know the truth have clothed it for the vulgar, and addressed the vulgar in the vulgar language and modes of conception, in order to convey part of the truth. (183)

Thus intelligent readers may be excused for saying, as Crabb Robinson said when he first read *Aids to*

[1] *L.S.*, ii. 68.

Reflection, that the 'philosophy seemed Coleridge's own, but that his religion seemed of the vulgar.' The last page of *Biographia*, when compared with the depths of the philosophical chapters, calls for the same kind of judgment.[1]

Nevertheless, the paradox cannot be excused away. It remains as a paradox, for which Coleridge is to be called to account only by those who hold him responsible for the errings of S.T.C. For this particular contradiction seems to me the clearest cut example of my main theme. Though it is impossible for a Coleridge to parody himself in such sentences as have been quoted, these religiosities are just of the kind to flourish in the soil of a character. Here is S.T.C.'s conservative care, what Mr. Muirhead calls the inveterate power of tradition over his mind. Here also is the sense of insufficiency, coupled with desire for recognition, especially (in view of quondam slights on his morals) for recognition from the devout; here is 'the exaggerated sense of his own mission as a renovator of the Christian religion, blown into a flame by the adulation of the more fanatical of his friends.'[2] Here finally is S.T.C. with his sense of guilt, and his desire to believe in a religion whose main tenet was the forgiveness of sins, affirming again and again that he cannot understand, but that he *feels*, that 'there is an original corruption in our nature . . . redeemable by Christ in a mysterious manner as an effect of his Crucifixion . . .'[3]

[1] *And of* C.'s *Confessio Fidei* (printed at the end of *Confessions of an Enquiring Spirit*):—'I believe in the life to come . . . because so to believe is my duty,' etc.
[2] J.H.M., 248.   [3] *U.L.*, i. 203.

Coleridge, on the other hand, reverses.
Item for item, Coleridge contradicts word and spirit
of S.T.C.

Coleridge on Christianity.

> I confess that till the light of the twofoldness of
> the Christian Church dawned on my mind . . . the
> study of the literature of the Church . . . infected
> me with a spirit of doubt and disgust. (*L.R.*, iv. 310)

Word and ritual are *not* one. Coleridge reserves his
especial eloquence and wit for false religion.

On mechanical religion:

> If acquiescence without insight; if warmth without
> light; if an immunity from doubt, given and guaran-
> teed by a resolute ignorance; if the habit of *taking
> for granted* the words of a catechism, remembered or
> forgotten; if a belief that seeks the darkness, and
> yet strikes no root, immovable as the limpet from
> the rock . . . (451)

and so to the completion of the period, better filled in
from a notebook:

> whereas to *doubt* has more faith, nay even to dis-
> believe, than that blank negation of all such thoughts
> and feelings which is the lot of the herd of church-
> and-meeting-trotters. (170)

As he decries habit-religion, so does he decry
enthusiasm-religion. He would have a selection from
the works of Swift and Butler of all passages that

'bear on Enthusiasm, Spiritual Operations, and pretences to the Gifts of the Spirit, with the whole train of New lights, Raptures, Experiences, and the like.'[1] He would stress the element of diverted sensuality in such manifestations, like a true modern, regretting particularly its results on 'nervous females,'[2] or describing false religion as 'arm in arm with sensuality on one side, and self-torture on the other.' He is rabid against cant terms in religion—doing things in a 'prayerful way,'[3] etc. He eloquently decries mere orthodoxy, as in his *Letters on the Inspiration of the Scriptures.*

On the false asceticism of false religion:

O how I abhor this abominable heart-haunting impurity in the envelope of modesty! (*L.R.*, iv. 360)

And on the conventional ethic and morality to which false religion gives rise:

I have not a deeper conviction on earth, than that the principles of taste and morals and religion which are taught in the commonest books of recent composition, are false, injurious and debasing.[4] (J.H.M., 26)

[1] 455.   [2] 697.   [3] 485
[4] I find Coleridge's simplest words on morality in a MS. (Add: 35, 343): 'written for whom I neither know nor care as a College Commemoration Sermon.

Wisdom of Solomon, iv. 16: Thus the Righteous that is dead shall condemn the Ungodly which are living.

There is a false and dangerous Philosophy which addresses itself to men, as to Beings of pure Intellect, and either forgets our Passions and affections, or argues for their Extinction. Instead of considering that as

And above all, Coleridge on the kind of religion which suits those who make a hobby out of controversy, or who try to advance the consciousness of God through the terms of logic. ('Religion has no speculative dogmas.'[1]) On those who argue for the inspiration of the Bible with 'pleadings fitter for an Old Bailey thieves counsellor than for a Christian divine.'[2] Using for their arguments 'logic, the rustling dry leaves of the lifeless reflex faculty.'

Religion in terms of Religion.

Yet who has ever thought of Coleridge as being wittily destructive of the religiose? Why is this attractive ability—and worse still why is Coleridge's true constructive religion—obscured by a few human lapses? The reason lies partly in the often noted distinction between Coleridge writing privately and Coleridge writing publicly, with the touch of orthodox solemnity he found necessary for the public occasion; partly in the fact that Coleridge in his religious writing associates himself with no novel expressions. He antagonises with conventional-looking titles and phraseology. There is no word like 'acceptance' or 'pragmatic' to attract by seeming to point invitingly down

---

moral Truth which is suited to the System of our Nature, the Professors of this Philosophy would fain suit the system of our nature to that which *they* consider as moral Truth . . . but . . . it is more than probable, that the System of Nature is wiser than their System of Philosophy; and were it not so, yet nature is certainly stronger . . . to attempt the removal of this intestine Dissension by exterminating all human Qualities, except Reason,—surely this were *clades, non medicina.* [1799]

[1] C.   [2] *L.R.*, IV. 5.

a trail clear of the worn old subject headings. He favours the usual religious terminology, so that with the capitalisations, and the tone of reverence too unremitting, the religious part of Coleridge's writings seems like something fit to be separated, something eminently avoidable, a Sunday subject.

Then, with the beginnings of thorough reading, this impression changes. 'Coleridge and Religion' becomes undetachable from 'Coleridge and Poetry' or 'Coleridge and Philosophy.' We begin to see how 'religion' is for Coleridge, as he sasy, 'the flower and crowning blossom of the plant,'[1] realising that when Coleridge uses the word 'blossom' he has in mind none of the buttonhole severability sometimes associated with the word. This flower is to be regarded, he goes on, as 'formed of whatever was most vital in root, stem, and leaf . . .' It stands for the clarifying of his life, the clarifying of Coleridge, the singling out of its radical strands, and the clearing of the way for their growth.

Against this kind of background of meaning the words of Coleridge's religious books, which we gaze at to start with unseeingly as we gaze at a parade of the once-great in a crowded museum, seem to come to life and to remove themselves by a whole world from the realm of religious orthodoxy which in their decay they most frequently inhabit. Again the paradox—it is necessary to know Coleridge completely before we know him at all. The following examples—restorations of meaning—must be taken as points significant only by virtue of their position on the surface

[1] J.H.M., 217.

of a sphere containing the experience of an individual. Coleridge himself supplies the prologue when he says:

> The slave of custom is roused by the rare and accidental alone; but the axioms of the unthinking are to the philosopher the deepest problems as being the nearest to the mysterious root and partaking at once of its darkness and pregnancy. (437)

Coleridge presents old axioms to demonstrate the value of the Bible, or of the Church, the importance of Revelation, or the desirability of Faith, in such a way that the insensitive bark each phrase has acquired in centuries of apathetic fingering is pulled away to reveal surprising green stem and acid sap below.

Thus does he present the Bible, which (a 'sun-dial by moonlight'[1] if read in the wrong way)

> above all contains a science of realities: and therefore each of its elements is at the same time a living germ, in which the present involves the future, and in the finite the infinite exists potentially.

*

> If in some gracious moment one solitary text of all its inspired contents should dawn upon us in the pure untroubled brightness of an idea. . . .

Thus he makes it seem possible once more to associate CHURCH, CHRISTIANITY, with something opposed to conformity, even in the sense of conformity to one

[1] S.M.

ideal: The value of the Church in England, he says, is that to every parish

> there is transplanted a germ of civilisation; that in the remotest villages there is a nucleus round which the capabilities of the place may crystallise and brighten. (467)

Crabb Robinson quotes Coleridge:

> There is no Church *of* England. We give a great advantage to the romanists by the expression—we should acknowledge only 'The Church *in* England.'

What Christianity can be follows from what the Church can be:

> What is Christianity at any one period? The Ideal of the Human Soul at that period. (*U.L.*, ii. 442)

Coleridge touches the stranded terms of religious controversy one by one, stirring them back into the liquids of meaning. In the days of early friendship with Poole, Coleridge had been a 'necessitarean.' Now he makes the word articulate. 'Logical and mathematical necessity subsist formally only. Real necessity is consciousness of the idea of God.'[1] In the same way he deformalises 'revelation' from its controversial meanings, describing it as a personal act. Our business, he says, is to reveal, to add to the body of revelation, not to derive it from—for instance—the *mythos* of the Jews.

Gradually the essentials of Coleridge's religion begin

[1] *S.M.*

to appear, essentials which are best summarised, I think, in an *Essay on Faith* printed at the end of the fourth volume of *Literary Remains*.

Faith, Coleridge says, is faith to our own selves. Unfaith comes from the drowning of this fidelity in the inundations of confused and immediate wishes: the momentary wish frustrates the workings of the permanent Will. Faith is, therefore, the mark of the more conscious man. Faith is the beginning of the kind of experience possible exclusively for man. 'The brutes' are capable of fealty. Men, only, of conscious fealty, which is faith.

Faith exists—with conscience, consciousness of faith, as witness—when the identity of the will and the reason is effected by the self-subordination of the will, or self, to the reason as representing the will of God.

It is impossible to separate 'Coleridge and Religion' from 'Coleridge and Philosophy.' 'Philosophy'—with postulate 'Know Thyself.' 'Religion'—his name for the pursuit of consciousness by disunited man, for the struggle of one Coleridge to contain, and by containing, to know and control a second irrelevantly diverging Coleridge. 'Struggle' is a symptomatic word here. Coleridge can restore meaning to the phrase *act of* faith. Faith, for him

> must be an energy . . . it must be a total, not a partial; a continuous, not a desultory or occasional energy. (438)

Thus are its own terms restored to Religion. In

bringing back reality to its phraseology, Coleridge re-inaugurates religious discussion. His conception of religion as a self-changing act is so far removed from the religious themes of his time, from Paley's evidences, Butler's analogy, or Warburton's ingenuities as to make it impossible to find any link by which both worlds of thought may be brought under the same heading. Coleridge gives back its value to the words 'mystery,' 'mystic.'[1] For his contemporaries, there was nothing in religion more mysterious than America was before Columbus discovered it. Now the spirit of Toland, maintaining that faith 'is entirely built upon ratiocination,' can be countered by Coleridge's 'I see now that what is spiritual can only be spiritually apprehended,' or Coleridge's version of St. Augustine's reply, when he was demanded the answer to one of the great 'religious questions' of the age:

I know it well enough when you do not ask me.[2]

'Subtlest hocus-pocus of "reason versus understanding"' Carlyle called it. Yet it is on the sincerity of Carlyle that suspicion falls as the completeness of this misunderstanding grows on us. Coleridge's 'reason' is especially relevant in this chapter. Turning over the old word, renewing it, he synonymises it with the 'spirit' of Paul and John, creating a new word out of the mutual fertilisation of two barren ones. Through his word he abolishes an arbitrary distinction between Coleridge-religion and Coleridge-

[1] *Cf.* p. 212.   [2] *C.S.*, 17.

philosophy, associating this key word of his philosophy, as he does, with his 'faith.' For the growth of consciousness, which for Coleridge is the 'end of our earthly being' he calls an 'act of reason.' Reason represents the gateway to consciousness, is *porta Dei in hominem aeternum.* Religion *is* reason, 'seen perspectively by a finite intellect.'[1]

'Act of faith,' 'act of reason'—philosophy, like religion, embodies for Coleridge an act. With his earlier heroes, with men like Hartley, there was an implication behind their philosophy of a general hopeful drift towards happiness; teaching showed how the painful element would be gradually absorbed by the pleasurable. The implied picture of life is of a world gradually *settling* into shape, knots being loosed; calmness, inertia, is the logical goal. But with the developed Coleridge it is all a clashing of opposites, passionate apprehensions, burstings out of chrysalis forms, breakings off from relationships grown stagnant.

Christ, Coleridge points out, is not described primarily and characteristically as a teacher, but as a doer. This truth is made truer in the process of knowing Coleridge, which involves knowing an enlargement of the meaning of the word 'do.'

Biographia Religiosa.

As footnote to this, for Coleridge readers less familiar with this element, a reminder of the difference of 'Coleridge on Religion' in early life and late.

In the sketch of Coleridge's development earlier

[1] 187.

in this book, a kind of religious evolution appeared. 'Happy godlessness' described Coleridge in the early 'nineties. Not that ever in his life he was unconcerned with religious matters, but at this time his concern was merely to be happily and athletically polemical in this field: violently emancipated in his creeds: selecting Unitarianism for its Left Wing properties: enthusiastically anti-superstition, anti-ritual:

> PRIEST, a name, after which any other term of abhorrence would appear an anti-climax. (429)

He ostentatiously refuses to have his first-born baptized. . . . But so far as the expression of a sense of God is concerned, this was confined to a poem or two—the *Æolian Harp,* for instance—and references to the 'one Life within us and abroad' . . . 'Rhythm in all thought and joyance everywhere.'

> Methinks it would have been impossible
> Not to love all things in a world so filled.

Coleridge is happy in action, including the fascinating pursuit of free-thinking theological discussion.

Then come his richest years, of extended experience, followed by the intellectual maturity to which the happy earlier years of 'bold' thought have been preface—increased powers of consciousness, which meant for him an increase of meaning to the word 'religion,' an increase not yet realised, suspected only. In 1800–4 Coleridge is giving us new meaning to Philosophy. Religion represents a further stage in articulation.

UNITY AND UNITARIANISM

But by 1802 not only has the cheerful godlessness gone, but pursuit of consciousness is no longer so bravely Coleridge's aim. With the conviction more and more obviously before him, that he is wasting his life, Coleridge begins to be a miserable sinner. He begins to turn to religion as one of the comforts, as I have described (p. 61 *ante*). All is now beginning to lead, as some hold, to nothing more than a final stage when Religion is the one subject, the monomania, with the notebooks nothing but theology, with Coleridge seeing himself as the renovator of the Christian religion, deeply involved at the same time in the coils of Trinitarian theology. Theological arguments once more, but now bitter: vehement attacks: denigration of past selves even. Sneers at his past happy certainty of an impersonal power:

> My state of mind was too often in too close a neighbourhood to the relaxing Malaria of the Mystic Divinity, which affects to languish after an extinction of individual consciousness—the sickly state which I had myself described in one of the Poems in the Sibylline Leaves, 'The Lover's Resolutions.' (*U.L.*, ii. 394)

Calling his past sense of an all-pervading spirit 'Pantheism' ('which—trick it up as you will—is but a painted atheism'[1]). Above all, turning on his youth, turning on the months when he was a Priestleian unitarian, and angrily blasting this also as 'atheism.'

The stages in this particular evolution can be

[1] *L.R.*, iv. 309.

summarised by three quotations on the subject of prayer.

In 1794, God is 'the Spirit . . .'

> Of whose omniscient and all-spreading Love
> Aught to *implore* were impotence of mind.

In 1797 (second edition of the poem) a Coleridge prophetic of a future self adds the footnote:

> I utterly recant the sentiment . . . my human reason being convinced of the propriety of offering *petitions* as well as thanksgivings.

Then, near the end of his life, it is more than a propriety:

> What a deathly *praeteritum perfectum* would the denial of prayer petrify the universe into.

But this picture of Coleridge's religious evolution is only one picture. It reflects, indeed, a process which was 'only elm, not oak' rooted in Coleridge.

One cause of the apparent swing to orthodoxy, for instance, is a change from a dislike of, to a taste for, the forms and ritual of religion. Very late in life Coleridge wrote:

> If an inscription be put upon my tomb, it may be that I was an enthusiastic lover of the church. (487)

And Coleridge did not mean by 'church' anything so abstract as to be above the *et ceteras* of church worship. There is doubtless something of an increasing physiological love of tradition here also.

The change is superficial, too, in another sense—in that this orthodoxy, as I have already shown, is applicable only to the all-too-human Coleridge, to S.T.C. I will try not to labour this point—but the exclusive choice of Anglican Christianity for a religion is perfectly characteristic of S.T.C. Such Christianity had so many attractions. It gave him a personal God. He left his unitarianism, his Deism, his Spinosistic 'intellectual love of God' for this very lack of the personal God which Anglican Christianity provided. ('My head was with Spinoza, though my whole heart remained with Paul and John.')[1] It taught him what he seemed to know, out of the depths of his self-disapproval, to be so demonstrably true—that 'slavery to the outer senses was base.' And then, to make up for the self-accusation entailed, it taught him the doctrine of redemption. Early in life Coleridge doubted this doctrine. Later he only wished to believe it. Later still, a strong 'presentiment'[2] developed. Towards the end of his life he seized on it. 'O what a miserable despairing wretch I should become,' he writes in a note, 'if I did not believe it . . .'[3]

Nevertheless this panic adoption of Christianity is only true of Coleridge down to a not very deep level. Side by side with this superficial Coleridge is another. In the very next paragraph to a page devoted to comforting tenets will come one of the true Coleridge apprehensions, true religion demonstrated in its own terms. Not far from the sentences on prayer just quoted will be found, perhaps, a true Coleridge defini-

[1] 242. [2] *U.L.*, i. 351. [3] *L.R.*, iv. 30.

tion of the same theme. 'Prayer,' he will be saying, 'is the effort to live in the spirit of the whole.'[1] Courageous action, instead of the world of comforts. All the time the real Coleridge, beneath the cloak, is realising his own Idea, is following the Religion which he defines as 'the binding of man's will to a will that is greater than itself.'

There is one mind, one omnipresent Mind

. . . with the which
Who feeds and saturates his constant soul,
He from his small particular orbit flies,
With blest outstarting! From himself he flies. . . .

To help him here, philosophy (which somewhere Coleridge says is no more and no less different from religion than the distinct is from the clear) is not enough. Through philosophy—to think of word-roots —he cannot, as through religion, *bind* himself. There is nothing in philosophy, he says, which will 'bind man's will' to a more essential will, so that it can revolve in a wider orbit:

if there is not the germ in the *Will*, which *is* the Individual in his essential individuality, which is deeper than our understanding . . . in vain the in-spiring Life, the fecundating Love. (*U.L.*, ii. 387)

This last from the final year, I believe, of Coleridge's life. No 'decay to orthodoxy' here.

[1] J.H.M., 37.

8

ANTICIPATION AND PROPHECY

Every principle contains in itself the germ of a prophecy.

ANTICIPATIONS

THERE is a strange letter of Coleridge's, written in 1814, a year when, in a decade of exculpations, he was particularly ready to defend himself. In this letter he airs a certain grievance, viz. that he has not received sufficient acknowledgment from his 'fellow-labourers in philosophical, political, and poetical literature.' He goes on to say that the science of reasoning and judging in these departments 'under PRINCIPLES, deduced from the nature of MAN, and that of prophesying concerning the future . . . by [a special process then enumerated] was as good as unknown in the public prints, before the year 1795–6.'[1] Then, in self-support, S.T.C. goes on to relate how he was able to say to Lord Darnley, 'I told you so.'

Thus, with full estecean ineptitude of tone, does Coleridge make a claim which is both superficially and radically true.

[1] 656.

Yet Coleridge is almost the last man whom the world goes to for the elucidation of a modern problem —for the comprehensible reason that his eighteentenishness is patent, his up-to-dateness negligible. The early nineteenth-century reflections in the levels of his verse: anti-regency puritanism, (*v. ante*): two or three similar characteristics of embryo Victorianism (Tennyson and the Keepsakes were coming in as Coleridge was going out): avidity for the discussion of small theological tenets (*v. ante*, p. 219: you do not now find leaders of thought who are keenly interested in the way 'Sherlock staggered to and fro between Tritheism and Sabellianism'): seeming political backwardness (*v. ante*): dislike of Reform Bills, dislike of political change.

On the other hand, in a somewhat less obvious but not much less superficial sense, Coleridge has some text-book importance as an anticipator of trends. Officially, in the world of official philosophy, he has a place as the first exponent of Modern Voluntary Idealism. There are religious connections, also, with the Oxford Movement. He is, all agree, the father of modern criticism, especially of modern Shakespeare criticism. More specifically, in the manner of our own decade or its immediate predecessor, it is the complexity of Shakespeare's characters which he reveals. It is the psychological aspect.

The 'psychological aspect' of Coleridge's work is the most obvious example of Coleridge as anticipator. He almost authorises the example himself.

... these are among the endless instances of the abject state to which psychology had sunk from the reign of Charles I to the middle of the present reign of George III; and even now it is but just awaking. (409)

Coleridge is prime instigator of its recovery, so that it is not surprising to find that much of modern psychological study takes its cast from him. Not only generally, formally, but in detail of exemplification. Many of the standard characters, the *drosophilæ* in the works of our contemporary Charles Dickenses, the psychopathologists, come straight from Coleridge. In my own copy I find noted such quotations as these. It is a by-word, he says, that 'religious enthusiasm borders on and tends to sensuality.' Yet it was not a by-word then. Or there are accounts of the trouble necessary to calm the rabid devoutness of unoccupied spinsters. If only Jer. Taylor, etc., would remember, he says, the effect that some of their works are likely to produce on 'nervous females under the irritation of Debility.' And there is the strange letter on sublimations (*L.*, 595) where he 'agrees' that 'chemistry in its present state tends to turn its priests into sacrifices. . . .' It is a substitute, he says, for love. 'We all have our obscure feelings, that must be connected with something or other—the miser with a guinea— Lord Nelson with a blue ribbon, Wordsworth's old Molly with washing-tub. . . . A miser *is in love* with a guinea. . . .' And note Coleridge's *method* in observing himself. ('I appear to myself like a sick physician, feeling the pang acutely, yet deriving a wonted pleasure from examining its progress and developing its causes.'[1]) Studying habits and motives with himself as subject. Studying *why* he has followed a certain train of thought; labouring over inconsistencies; trying to find reasons—very near modern psychology this— *why* he habitually mis-writes or forgets certain words. And on the whole describing character unhandicapped by the insincerity of the conventional moral judgment, in spite of his own estecean sense of guilt, in spite of theologies dear to the Coleridge family. 'It is well to have a general suspicion of ourselves,' he is able to say, 'in the moment of an inclination to advise.'[2]

But if anyone doubts that Coleridge was able to transcend the moral standards of his time and was able not to conform his criticisms with the moral ideal of a good man, it is more certain, and much more important, that he was able to transcend our contemporary tendency, the tendency of contemporary psychology, to substitute the moral standard of a normal man. For Coleridge psychology—and here comes the core of the problem 'Coleridge as Prophet'—does more than anticipate. In Coleridge's psychology are the elements which divide him, as a seer, from reverend tipsters, and philosophical long-view men. Which divide him, with absolute difference, from his modern psychological disciples. Coleridge psychology is not our psychology.

PROPHECIES

The Coleridge man, like the Freudian man, is possessed of depths below the surface. But these depths

[1] *L.,* 107.   [2] 596.

contain something more than that which has been Freudianly pushed there. That is the limit of our profundity now, the extent of our mystery; superficialities pushed into the shallows. These Coleridge depths descend to roots from which true differentiation springs. Coleridge's vision of man is of differences not comprehensible by observation of behaviour. When Coleridge says 'how much lies *below* consciousness,'[1] he. is not thinking, as we might be, of an old curiosity shop of symbolical lumber, rings, horns, church steeples, and the like. He is thinking of the vast and varied structures, the huge potential differences, in men.

Coleridge, standing at the beginning of the psychological epoch, inaugurating it, seems almost alone to have psychologised from life. If anatomy presupposes a corpse, as D'Annunzio says, modern psychology presupposes a marionette. With Coleridge, psychology is not a method of grouping similarities and explaining away eccentricities: it is a question of knowing differences, in order to give free play to the correlatives of those differences as they exist in the self. . . . 'It is only a question of attitude'—true. But Coleridge's attitude, the premise from which he starts, is his own creation, and part of the unique Coleridge 'quality.'

A prophet is the man who transmits his own quality to the world. If this is a true proverb, Coleridge is a true prophet. The great writer will always have some distinctive attitude to life. But mere attitude always

----
[1] 161.

represents a point of view, a point on the surface of the sphere; and if the sphere is as large as the world, this view, instead of appearing as it is tangential only, will seem to range over an infinite plane, so that there is likely to grow up a false impression that the world is flat. The great man supplies the missing dimension. He has not a point- but a radius-of-view, joined to the centre. He knows the world not by external contemplation, but by radial possession. Instead of an attitude to life, there is a new relation to life, a new quality in life, which his work will express. His radial line starts a new direction. Coleridge describes this in another way when he gives as an example of genius (as opposed to talent) the power of 'modifying a series of thoughts by some one predominant thought or feeling,'[1] or saying that 'images become proofs of original genius only so far as they are modified by a predominant passion.'[2]

It is difficult to find words for the Coleridge 'quality.' 'Coleridge' is intangible, as S.T.C. is blatant. I once thought that I knew this quality perfectly. It had something to do with Mrs. Browning's vague word for him—'visionary,' was itself vague; the words 'Poetic genius' came in, light that never was, unearthly glare of moonlight. But in retrospect I see that this notion of C., which is a rather usual one, was founded in my case on a good first-hand knowledge of his famous poems and a second-hand knowledge of his 'mystical philosophy.' In the process of knowing Coleridge, this preconception of him as

[1] 255.   [2] 257.

'vague' becomes reversed. One of his habits most obviously in contradiction is a tendency to concern himself very urgently with objects and facts not in themselves usually considered important. 'He interests himself so much about every little trifle,' as Dorothy Wordsworth said. A concentric rather than an eccentric habit. A random page from the Gutch notebook will reflect this, or from any later MS. book. In Eg. 2800 he notes down concentrations on the format of a monthly magazine . . . points on the queen's trial . . . weather forecasting by bird behaviour . . . the walk and gestures of two lovers—each subject taken up with as earnest a return to first principles as if comprehensive treatment was actually decided upon.

Yet the Coleridge quality has nothing to do with factual, objective detail. It has something to do with 'concrete,' with 'real,' but not the kind of reality which is easily comprehensible. Perhaps the key lies in this very lack of objectivity. It is not the many, but the one, which Coleridge expresses. Something impels Coleridge to the root from which the many spring. There is a letter of 1797 in which he speaks of this. From my early reading, he says,

> my mind had been habituated *to the Vast*, and I never regarded my *senses* in any way as the criteria of my belief. . . . Those who have been led to . . . truths step by step, through the constant testimony of their senses, seem to me to want a sense which I possess. They contemplate nothing but *parts*. . . . And the universe to them is but a mass of *little things*. (532)

Very likely, Coleridge is wrong in his diagnosis. He is certainly aware of the 'little things,' and it may be his vivid apprehension of them which gives him his knowledge of the whole. 'All things wait in all things.' But in his ideas, in his descriptions, in his characterisations of Shakespeare's characters, in his worrying over the idiosyncrasies of S.T.C., in his knowledge of Coleridge, the root is implied. He writes *with reference to* the whole, the root of roots, the idea idearum, the semina seminarum. 'Radical' may be the word, though perhaps 'source' contains a better metaphor. He does not fix, in his descriptions or pronouncements: he dissolves. He stirs long stagnant thoughts back into the stream, so that they are in reviving contact once more with the source. It may be 'Coleridge,' it may be 'S.T.C.,' who unlike most poets and creators is incapable of the detail of his world. 'Sloth, carelessness, resignation in all things that have reference to mortal life is not merely *in* me, it is me.'[1] True, obviously, of the world of Coleridge and mundane detail; but for the truth of Coleridge and the world of life, each word must be reversed.

The dissolving, superseding force of this Coleridge quality, its subversive powers, and therefore its prophetic powers, can best be seen by placing it up against the intellectual background of Coleridge's own age. Coleridge is generally regarded as fitting well into his period, if only as early romantic. But in respect of his true 'quality,' there is no fit at all. 'Coleridge' is in complete opposition to his own time.

[1] *U.L.*, i. 269.

The intellectual climate, the habit of thought, against which to preserve his integrity the individual had to fight in 1800, had a very different name from that which thwarted the first men of the renascence. These earlier pioneers were opposed by the Church, which meant rigorous concealments, esoteric learning, cornerings up of the instruments of knowledge, wielding of power through the apparatus of superstition—forces of darkness. In 1800 there is a different kind of enemy. The Old Whig is the New Tory. Enlightenment and Emancipation have conquered. Enlightenment, blazing in the imagination of Dantes and Giottos, expressed in action by Galileos and Francis Bacons, expressed in words by Chaucer and Rabelais, has burnt itself out, and the age of Reason comes. The great emancipation is petrified into a permanent statue of liberty. In turn, the age of Reason itself decays into a new but maggoty liveliness, into the age of Logic, and intrepid pamphleteers are attacking beliefs which have been settled with for two hundred years, till they are fixed for ever in the attitude of boldly calling spades spades. In more precise and less rhetorical terms, and with more special reference to England and Coleridge in this year 1800, the thought, ethic, metaphysic, religion of the country, the tastes of its young men, and the general intellectual climate (capable of being tested, in any age, Coleridge has pointed out, by noting the 'anticipated sympathies' of its literature) is, under the autocracy of Reason, decayed into common sense. The new instrument of Francis Bacon has been philosophised prosaically by

Locke, impersonally by Hume, and ludicrously by the Beatties. It is translated into invincibly everyday life by Dr. Johnson: turned into a bizarre ethic by the Paleys of the time. The Romantic taste of the period —for graves, moats, ghosts, ruins, ballads, and Ossian— is of course only a taste, garniture to counteract the dry flavour of the omnipresent common sense. The rush for Mrs. Radcliffe and Byron represents a substitute in the world of fantasy for the realities which common-sense standards either avoided, or ineffectively attempted to deal with in its own terms. Nothing is more symptomatic of the Age of Logic than the taste for the Romantick. Coleridge came to consciousness in a world where the tone of thought seemed always to stop short of reality on the side of the worldly, just as the artistic taste overstept it into the fantastic.

Not only the tone of thought, but the issues themselves. The highly common-sense problems of freewill versus necessity. Atheism versus deism. Deism versus Christianity. The subjective idealism question. Or the question of Miracles. The subjects of dispute, the particular lifeless rocks on which opponents chose to split themselves, label the age. Coleridge himself is to be found discussing miracles with Poole, the first proto-friend. There still exists a note by Poole of some of the themes. But it is un-Coleridgean—Poole has summarised it under the unbelievable contemporary headings.[1] This particular subject, and the way it was treated by the age, is a good illustration of the ludicrous results of the treatment by Logic of subjects

[1] *Cf.* L.S.

beyond its scope. A strange aspect of such controversies is the way in which the arguments of the protagonists can be summarised in one unsubtle sentence. Those of the famous Woolston, for instance, whose conclusions were that the miracles must be allegorical, not to say fictitious, because to believe the stories 'exceeded all power of face.' Collins, who proved that there must be some mistake somewhere. Bishop Smalbroke, who answered Woolston and vindicated the New Testament by quoting Arnobius to the effect that the devils were in a state of special activity about the time of Christ's coming. Sherlock, who with detective powers more suited to Watson or Lestrade, demonstrates the unanimity of apostle witnesses. Annet, who proves them guilty of perjury. If a man tells me, said Annet, that he jumps over the River Thames, I know the story to be a lie, and trouble myself no more about it. Even Hume concerned himself, explaining without scorn but with perfection of irrefutability that of course no evidence can prove a miracle. In general, the leaders of the eighteenth century expended their powers in being brilliantly scornful, like Voltaire, of the miracle upholders. They thought themselves bold in demolishing men like Waterland, upholder of the literal truth of the Word, who showed how God, in order to bring off the first rainbow, kept clouds and water from making rainbow formation before that date. Gibbon and Horace Walpole were 'Middletonians,' holding that miracle stories showed nothing but the credulity of the narrator —surely in no other age would so unstriking a tenet be found gloriously attached to any one man's name. *Cf.* 'Tillotsonian.' To be a Tillotsonian on the subject of Transubstantiation was to hold that the doctrine was contrary to the evidence of the senses. This was not Tillotson's only piece of intellectual valour. He was brave enough to say, with reference to that other subject so obviously suited to logical treatment, the doctrine of the Trinity, that if all the great Mathematicians in the world told him that 2 plus 2 did not equal 4 he would not believe them. How much less likely would he be likely to give credence to the statement made by men who were in no sense mathematicians, that 3 equalled one? Gibbon is Tillotsonian as well as Middletonian. He dates a crucial phase in his development from the time when, as a convert to Catholicism, he noticed that the blood of Christ did not taste like the blood of Christ but was supposed to be the blood of Christ. And so on and so on— the atmosphere seems hypnotic. Indeed the words of the heterodox are not less ludicrous than the words of the orthodox—are the same, because the problems are the same, with the same fallacy always present in the treatment—the application of Logic to subjects not susceptible of such treatment. The problems of ethics and philosophy all followed these lines. A Blake could thrive audaciously independent of this atmosphere, but of the four or five who had heard of Blake there would be a million who revered Paley, or admired Beattie for refuting the atheism of Hume by saying that the soul must be distinct from the body, because he had never heard of any nation that denied it.

And to all this the Coleridge quality was opposed. Implicitly and explicitly, the Coleridge quality runs counter to the 1800 attitude.

Implicit opposition, for instance, in the ability of Coleridge to be serious.

The eighteenth century was serious enough in its own way. But the seriousness is uneasily interposed, turned on, has now to us an air of period which makes it farcical, whether it is Robinson Crusoe discoursing on morals, or Prince Rasselas on the vanity of human wishes, or Blair, Gray, Radcliffe, lingering in the graveyard. Even the real leaders of thought, like Hume, seem to be just off true seriousness, just off a real issue, philosophising from a philosophy, moralising from an ethic, instead of from experience. It is true that in his careless or estecean moments the seriousness of Coleridge has the eighteenth-century 'graver moment' atmosphere. But on the true Coleridgean days it is weightless and invigorating, an athletic profundity; it is the de-paralysis of our consciousness of some issue which truly affects us.

Coleridge on seriousness:

> O! it requires deeper feeling, and stronger imagination, than belongs to most of those, to whom reasoning and fluent expression have been as a trade learnt in boyhood, to conceive with what *might*, with what inward *strivings* and *commotion*, the perception of a new and vital TRUTH takes possession of an uneducated man of genius. (*B.L.*, i. 197)

Oppose to this Coleridge's own age as he himself

summarises it. 'There is now no reverence for anything,' he says, 'and the reason is, that men possess
conceptions only, and their knowledge is conceptional
only.' For reverence is only possible, he says, towards
ideal truths, meaning, by 'ideal,' formulated from
crucial and self-changing experience. Coleridge's attitude to the age of Reason from which he was escaping
could be paradoxed by saying that he thought it
deficient in the very faculty after which it was named.
Citing Hume's *History* as an example, he discourses
on 'the inadequacy of the mere understanding to the
apprehending of moral greatness.'[1] Hume 'accounts
for' the efforts of heroic spirits by such motives as
selfishness, etc. The judgments of the understanding,
Coleridge would say, are lessening judgments. Coleridge is generally patronising of Goethe's *Faust*, but
he agrees that if he had written it himself his devil
also would have represented Satan by virtue of being
the universal humorist, a man of the understanding
only, without the faculty of Reason, in whose field
pleasures and pains became unreal, the universal
lessener.[2] And just as he gives back active force to the
word 'Reason,' so was Coleridge to restore to its
original dignity the word 'enthusiasm,' which for a
hundred years had been no better than a term of
abuse. 'Nothing great,' he says, 'was ever achieved
without enthusiasm. For what is enthusiasm but the
oblivion and swallowing up of self in an object dearer
than self, or in an idea more vivid?'[3] Coleridge brought
back the possibility of belief without the fanaticism

[1] *S.M.*   [2] 503.   [3] *S.M.*

which involves the swallowing up of the object in the self.

Perhaps this implicit opposition of Coleridge (and his explicit, fiercely polemical opposition as well): his apparent subservience to some of the trends of his time: his gift of predicting our present, and his power of prophesying, of imagining, our future, are best epitomised under another heading, namely, *Coleridge and Science.*

Coleridge had long-standing connections with science. As a boy, science came early into the field of his violent curiosity; interest developed through the help of a surgeon brother, whose medical books he read, and whose experiments he learnt something of. His later 'extraordinary interest' in 'every little thing' was preliminary to his scientist's study of cause and effect in nature. A.D.S. summarises this part of Coleridge's activity from the point of view of his interest in medical controversies. All through his life, the most regularly recurring note in his commonplace books is concerned with an experiment or an observation. Galvanism — electricity — animal magnetism. The comments are sometimes valuable in themselves-- what he says about cloud types in *A.P.*, for instance, or the flight of birds in the margins of the British Museum copy of White's *Selborne.* Sometimes the comment is estecean:

It would be singularly desirable to try the effect of animal magnetism on a sick Indian. (MS. Eg. 2800, f. 88)

After 1800, when Coleridge's powers of new apprehension were beginning to decline, the time had come for him to co-ordinate the experience of precedent years. Full of knowledge, he desired science as a more ordered way of knowing, turning to it deliberately, associating this new move in his life, as usual, with a new friend (Humphry Davy. *Cf. ante* p. 48). As soon as he came up against such irrelevancies as the need for systematic application, his immediate keenness, of course, evaporated. But Coleridge had his foot more deeply in science for the rest of his life. He squared science with his own self-created world. What he has to say about it is one of the keys to that world.

In the realm of science there are two forces, one positive and the other negative. The positive force is represented by the true scientist, the poet-scientist, who apprehends objects, and imagines new relations between them; the negative force is the dogmatism which congeals in the wake of the true scientists. It is the scientific attitude. It calmly collects, accounts for and summarises data in terms of the laws which the true scientists create. Coleridge, if he had broken his habit of life and carried his science proclivities through to a consummation, might himself have been the true scientist of his era. There are signs. There are suggestions in his notebooks, for instance, that he could *initiate* experiment, attempt a cosmogony in his own terms (*cf.* A.D.S. on 'Coleridge's Cosmogony'), imagine new relations—*e.g.* in plants, to quote from MS. Eg. 2800 (as far as I can decipher it):

'The plant is the nuptial garland of Earth and Air—the equation of Carbon, Oxygen and Hydrogen. Or as Carbon is the negative factor of Life, is common to all the realms of organic nature, we may better call the Vegetable Tribe the equation of Oxygen and Hydrogen, not the neutralisation which is Water. . . . In the flower, we have the qualitative product of Oxygen = Light in the outness and splendor of Colors, the qualit: prod: of Hydrogen = Warmth in the inwardness and sweetness of Fragrances.' Perhaps a true realist-scientific suggestion, with none of what Coleridge calls somewhere the 'abstraction of the analysed plant.' He was in no way bound to the science of his own age. Even mediæval astrology, product of what Coleridge denominated 'the so-called dark ages,' he could see to be only a too-logical following out of a finely imagined truth:

It is curious to mark how instinctively the reason has always pointed out to men the ultimate end of the various sciences, and how immediately afterwards they have set to work, like children, to realise that end by inadequate means. . . . There is no doubt but that astrology of some sort or other would be the last achievement of astronomy: there must be chemical relations between the planets; . . . but this, though, as it were, blindly and unconsciously seen, led immediately to fortune-telling and other nonsense. So alchemy is the theoretic end of chemistry. (498)

In a period when science was at a low ebb, chemistry feeble, and geology (except for Hutchinsonians collecting fossils in order to try to prove the date of the Flood) non-existent, Coleridge went straight to the one true scientist, Davy, concerned himself with the one scientific philosophy of value, what was then called vitalism, and evolved the one valid evolutionary principle, the principle of individuation (*cf. ante*, p. 192). Coleridge knew, and was able to define, true science. Science is power, he says, because it consists wholly in ideas and principles, and 'every principle is actualised by an idea; and every idea is living, productive, partaketh of infinity, and (as Bacon has sublimely observed) containeth an endless power of semination.' Thus in the language of *The Statesman's Manual*. More colloquially in his notebooks:

> The first man of science was he who looked into a thing, not to learn whether it could furnish him with food, or shelter, or weapons, or tools, or ornaments, or *playwiths*, but who sought to know it for the gratification of *knowing*; while he that first sought to *know* in order to *be* was the first philosopher. (186)

And then as text-book of this kind of knowing for the sake of knowing, Coleridge proffers the Bible: 'All other sciences are confined to abstractions (*e.g.* the abstraction of the analysed plant). . . . The Bible alone contains a science of realities; and therefore each of its elements is at the same time a living germ, in which the present involves the future, and in the finite the infinite exists potentially.'[1] The seed, once more, of a Novum Organum.

[1] *S.M.*

So much for the creations of Coleridge as a scientist. Further quotations could be taken from certain letters, from Notebooks, *Statesman's Manual*, and the post-humously published *Hints Towards the Formation of a More Comprehensive Theory of Life*. What Coleridge has to say in militancy of the negative aspect of the world of science, the scientific attitude, is more easily quoted, and more easy to read.

The philosophy of the attitude he calls mechanico-corpuscular:

> With the Restoration came in all at once the mechanico-corpuscular philosophy, which made everything in philosophy, religion, and poetry objective; till, at length, attachment to mere external worldliness and forms got to its maximum. (497)

Its logic he calls syllogistic:

> There are two kinds of logic: 1. Syllogistic. 2. Criterional. How any one can by any spinning make out more than ten or a dozen pages about the first, is inconceivable to me; all those absurd forms of syllogisms are one half pure sophisms, and the other half mere forms of rhetoric. (493)

Its ethic he criticises on the ground that it cancels individuality for the sake of an abstraction, 'mankind.' To the logical question, Would not the World function as well, be the same, if run on principles of enlightened selfishness as opposed to what Coleridge calls 'the

255

unconditional obedience of the Will to the pure
Reason?' Coleridge answers: 'All possibly might
remain the same, only not the men themselves.'

*

All the great—the permanently great—things that
have been achieved in the world, have been so
achieved by individuals . . . the rage now-a-days is
all the other way . . . for organisations.

*

The exponent of mechanico-corpuscular Coleridge
calls 'the pollarded man'—clipped, as we should say,
of a dimension. Pollarded and unpollarded are almost
his prime categories for mankind:

Every man is born an Aristotelian, or a Platonist.
They are the two classes of men, beside which it is
next to impossible to conceive a third. (471)

Coleridge himself could understand what he called
the 'Aristotelian' so well: Coleridge, who had been so
hard bound in the spells of materialist philosophy as a
young man, who had allowed himself to be so fascinated
by the homeliness, the prettiness, of machine explanations of the workings of the soul. Once he himself had
swarmed into the works of Hume and Priestley. His
earliest friends were limited to men of the common-
sense dimensions—Southey, for instance, and Hazlitt.
And Coleridge had always warm admiration, and

even fellow-feeling, for such permanently emancipated men as Godwin, or Thelwall. He well knew the value of the impulse to enlighten, though he may not have been thinking that it was his part to serve thus. '*Do you*,' he writes to Thelwall, 'uplift the *torch* dreadlessly, and show to mankind the face of that idol which they have worshipped in darkness.'[1] But for Coleridge, the breaking of the idol and the loosening of the chains was only the first step.

*

What in all this makes Coleridge a modern prophet? The word 'modern'—in the sense of looking forward to the future—calls lazily to mind some newspaper series: *A.D. 2034 . . . men in air-suits . . . precipitous sky-scrapers . . . ankle deep in speed tracks, their heights obscured by thrusting and clustering aircraft.* Or the gently directed thoughts may lead to a brave new world of bravely *logical* laws, pleasures, organisations, or to sexless Ancients, half-way to becoming vortices of pure cogitation. But let the thoughts be questioned sternly and they will have to admit that this kind of future—of speed, factorylessness, asepsis, and parthenogenesis—is not the future at all, but the world of the past. Is pendent to Francis Bacon, and the first men of the renascence. Is the logical extension of the past, not the unpredictable future. The real future cannot be successfully foretold by studying intellectual or cultural tendencies. The future *grows* from the present; it does

[1] *L.*, 194.

not accrete, it is created, by the true scientists, the true poets, the prophets.

Obviously, Coleridge is not most notably prophet in the sense that he tipped forthcoming events or foreshadowed tendencies which now stand out clearly, even if he is the father of modern psychology. But he is a prophet in the sense that he created his own world, a world which, in spite of our need of a changed intellectual and spiritual atmosphere, we have not yet begun to incorporate. Indeed, the forces opposed to growth and new differentiation are the same now as they were in Coleridge's time; the sterilising habit is still the religion of enlightenment-and-emancipation, more potent now than ever, because linked up till lately with a valuable and necessary reaction against Victorian superstition, with modernity, and with a sweet and limber ethic of progress and evolution. So that there is a modern utilitarianism, a modern mechanico-corpuscular philosophy, more potent because more universally understood, a modern vibratiuncle theory of the emotions, and mechanical explanations of the differences between men, more rigid even than those formulated by pollarded Humes or lopped successors of Ben Jonson, and more in need than ever of reviving draughts of Coleridge psychology. There is a modern Age of Reason attitude, a scientific attitude, a very undivine detachment, in the face of which all that Plato and Goethe stand for have little meaning, and struggles of the human soul for full expression appear as the misfunctioning of badly made parts in the machine. It is true that in theory all take it for granted that 'individuality' is good, and that just at present to speak regretfully of the mechanisation of life evokes murmurs of agreement. But by mechanisation of life seems generally to be meant the mechanisation of machines (with their undeniably non-human qualities). And efforts to counteract mechanisation seem to be directed not towards ourselves but towards these innocent engines: gasometers will be thatched, Redline and Ethyl will be poured from spouts modelled in imitation of the parish pump, we cry out as if in pain when we see the tender grey gleam of a distant pylon on the hillside. This strange mistake seems to show a consciousness somewhere of a handicapping mechanisation in our natures, but our heroes are still the emancipators, the 'anticipated sympathies' of our time all point to a desire for more and more common-sense books, scientific books, cause-and-effect books, with the cause always a boldly or amusingly shocking 'give away' of an effect of ancient magnificence. Our leaders are still resolutely concerned in calling spades spades, even though they do not show an equal courage to call souls souls, or the greatness of the human spirit greatness. Man's superb powers of consciousness are used for the purpose of making catalogues or genealogical tables, so that, as Coleridge says, the light that lighteneth every man tends to dwindle into 'the light of a glow-worm, by which he can distinguish one reptile from another.'[1]

Coleridge does not show a route away from the common-sense age, either forward to completer

[1] *C.S.*, 188.

common senses, or 'back to nature.'[1] He objectifies the attitude: sees all round materialism: has once himself, in his notion stage, been confined, thought and word, to its terms: knows it, therefore, for what it is—the introduction to thought, the bud of thought, the clear-cut, temptingly simplified first stage in expression. His attacks are not directed against this stage, once part of himself, but against its unnatural prolongation. He was surrounded then, as we are now, by men whose growth had stopped short, men transfixed for ever in the attitude of beginning to know, so in love with their first contact with the world of knowledge that they lived on the reminiscence of their pristine feelings and made heroes of the writers who struck in them that glorious first spark, making them 'ever after fetish.'

Coleridge objectifies the attitude as a stage in the evolution of the individual. And Coleridge the Prophet is revealed here because the evolution of the individual, the phenomenon of post-physical growth, the power to differentiate, and to continue to differentiate, is not yet consciously the problem. 'Individualism' is associated with an unpleasant kind of economic. The primary meaning of 'self-consciousness' and 'self-seeking,' the everyday significance, is still bad. It is

---

[1] We are reminded that C. is not our sort of scientist by such sentences as these: 'The savage state is a temporary accident as of ship-wreck, Migration, or Flight before a conqueror, especially where that Flight is accompanied with Dispersion. So far from being the state of Human *Nature* and of course the original State of Man, it is of all states the most unnatural of Man, because it is the most inhuman.' (MS. Eg. 2800, f. 94).

now more than ever an age of groups, federations, national movements for war, international movements for peace: Men do not exist, only Mankind. Coleridge stands for Men. He himself is a separate, individual Man by virtue of the 'neat little world within him' which he describes, wherein light exists as 'on the third day of creation, before it was polarised into outward and inward,' and he is a prophet by virtue of the possession of this world of as yet uncreated life, without the being and working of which, he says, the world to come, the future, would be 'either as unintelligible as *abracadabra*, or a mere reflection and elongation of the world of sense—Jack Robinson between two looking-glasses.' (*Is not nature prophetic up the whole vast pyramid of organic being?*)[1] Coleridge also would have had the right to say 'I am the acme of things accomplished, the encloser of things to be.' Coleridge is a prophet not by virtue of any onward-pointing, oracular finger; he is a prophet because his contact makes for difference, keeps the varying directions of men separate. His hard-won evolution, his perilous explorations of the least accessible depths of the self, his perpetual struggle to resist the averaging, standardising restraints of his character, makes him the prophet of the new world of individuals.

'Mankind does not exist, only Men.' This phrase is Goethe's. I wish some celestial B.Litt. or Ph.D. candidate would choose as his thesis not 'Coleridge and Schelling,' 'Coleridge and Schlegel,' but 'Cole-

[1] These quotations are taken from Coleridge's most profound, most unreprinted 'Dialogue between Demosius and Mystes.'

ridge and Goethe.' He will have the mountainous labour he lusts for, because not only will his reading have to be enormous, his skill in the technique of clarification subtle, but he will have to acquire the poet's capacity for experience and the true philosopher's knowledge of men. In the two characters, in biographical details, he will find nothing but contrast. He will have to go to the root, to the perhaps only intuitively comprehensible centres of both men, before he finds in Goethe Coleridge's only contemporary 'like'—homomorph (if that is the word); and then he will see what to the future will be a commonplace, Coleridge and Goethe standing alone as prophets of the age which will have succeeded them.

TRANSCENDENTALISM
EXPLAINED

A NOTE ON MR. I. A. RICHARDS'
COLERIDGE ON THE IMAGINATION

VERY unfortunately for me, Mr. Richards' book on Coleridge came out when these essays were already with my publishers, too late for me to be able to make use of it. A first reading has made me wish to revise some of my pages, notably those on which I talk about Coleridge's relations with his own vocabulary (*cf.* note, p. 175); nevertheless I would not, even if it were possible, alter or eliminate paragraphs in which I find myself trying to say the same things as Mr. Richards even when I have said them with less precision. This because, not in spite of, the wide difference in the worlds, cultural and otherwise, of Mr. Richards and myself, and a certain interest which thereby attaches to these coincidences.

I should like to take advantage of the note-character of this appendix to murmur over my first unorganised thoughts on Mr. Richards' important book.

I believe that the average reader, knowing perhaps the gist of Mr. Richards' *Principles of Criticism*, its vocabulary, its points of attack and its admirable clarifications was prepared to be scandalised by his book on Coleridge. I, for instance, knew that Mr. Richards had anatomised mercilessly—dissected to death, as one hopes—the 'literary' critics of our own time, revealing sometimes interiors too marshy even to be analysed. I knew that with these things went not only less negative merits, but a love of a certain kind of detachment, of words like 'emotive' and other things emotive in me of an emotional dislike of the 'scientific attitude,' the common-sense attitude, with which they are usually associated. Would, Mr. Richards criticise Coleridge from this point—Coleridge, so laudably vulnerable to such treatment, and all its irrelevantly lessening effects? To summarise Mr. Richards in one of his own sentences, it seems his work is motivated by the belief that the 'theory of literary analysis is . . . on the point of making, through experiment, those contacts with actuality that would transform it into a science, and a science from which very important practical utilities may be expected to result.' 'Important practical utilities.' There seems too much acerbity of restraint about this ideal to recommend a critic about to dedicate himself to the exposition of so great a spirit. Mr. Richards has stared so often, and with such parching effect, at attempted analyses of the great by the less great; we have enjoyed with him so many grim inquiries into the ambiguities of critics made vague from their lack of clear feelings; he subjects to so merciless a quiz the private likes and dislikes of nice old parties, and dashing but fallible younger members: now, if his attack has been only a method of defence, now when he is dealing exclusively with the great, the inside of Mr. Richards will be exposed for criticism. But would-be critics of Mr. Richards, if these exist, will find that he is not a negative critic here. He enlarges Coleridge for us. Because Mr. Richards has something important to say about Coleridge, he actually dispenses with S.T.C. altogether, making me, for instance, wonder if I was right to take up a third of my own book pointing the characteristics and separate existence of this irrelevant figure. 'Coleridge on the Imagination' is shown here as pure 'Coleridge,' building a philosophy on experience, on self-discovery; elaborating principles so that the remoter areas of the new conquests can be more thoroughly explored (re-presented here with certain elements still further clarified by Mr. Richards to that same end). Mr. Richards concentrates on what 'Coleridge' means by 'feeling,' by 'reason,' by 'good sense'; he describes 'Coleridge' knowing and being.

It seems to me, however, that Mr. Richards is personally concerned in the omission of an important element from his discussion of 'Coleridge on the Imagination.' And it seems to me that the cause of this omission—consciously made by Mr. Richards—is worth trying to understand.

I remember having read on some announcement connected with this book, or on a dust-cover, that Coleridge's evolution was to be described; I was disappointed to see these words in the introduction:

> I have not tried to sort out the strands in any *historical* fashion. That would be a more difficult venture in interpretation, and at present premature.

It is certainly true that the detail of Coleridge's evolution will never be known clearly until all the notebooks are made accessible and their contents chronologically arranged. It is one of the most important pieces of English editing which still wants doing. But the broad lines of this evolution have been long known, from the letters and notes which have already been published, and have been successfully analysed, first by Shawcross, later by Muirhead. And since Coleridge is one of the very few 'great English writers' who have been capable of a history more important than a history of births, deaths, and marriages it may be regretted that Mr. Richards has not at any rate made use of the facts to hand, even if he has not re-assembled it in the light of his valuable knowledge and critical powers. If, as he himself says, the 'know thyself' postulate of Coleridge's philosophy is an act of growth, if 'feeling' and 'knowing' mean for him acts of growth, why have they not been so described?

How, in fact, does he describe these changes in Coleridge? How, for instance, does he describe what he truly presents as the greatest change in Coleridge, the change from the Hartleian, necessitarean Coleridge to the Coleridge of 1802, the change from the Coleridge regarding philosophy as a game in the pursuit of which pleasing mechanical explanations may be invented for the external world, to the Coleridge who regards philosophy as an individual creation, a deepening consciousness of the hitherto unfathomed, with postulate 'know thyself'? Citing the relevant quotations, Mr. Richards describes it thus:

By the middle of March [1901] the great change had happened and Coleridge was well launched.

*

The passage from the conception of the mind's doings as Fancy to that of the creative Imagination is the passage from Hartley to Kant.

*

. . . Coleridge's conversion from Hartley to Kant.

It seems to me that the word 'conversion' thus slipped in does not turn up by chance. Mr. Richards uses the word because he really denies the fact of *growth*, he really does not know these changes from the point of view of development, of the increasing differentiation in the life of an individual. A youth is not *converted* when he changes his naked upper lip to a downy one.

Seeking for an explanation of this enigma, I remember a phrase from Mr. Richards' first chapter, which on first reading I had taken as amusingly paradoxical, rather than as a serious statement. *A propos* Coleridge's famous and by him often-repeated division of mankind into Aristotelians and Platonists, Mr. Richards, after suggesting 'Materialist and Idealist' as alternative terms, goes on to say:

I write then as a Materialist trying to interpret before you the utterances of an extreme Idealist. . . .

Coleridge is to be explained in terms of Materialism.

It may be that the reader will see nothing strange in this assertion: nor is there. Materialists are chiefly celebrated for their explanations of what may loosely be called non-material characters. What would be interesting would be to see Coleridge subjected to a treatment against the limitations of which his whole life and philosophy are opposed, and from a man who must know all the arguments against such treatment, if only from his sympathetic knowledge of his Coleridgean theme.

The reader will be thinking that Mr. Richards' most unportentously made suggestion ought not to be taken so seriously. But in his phrasing of it he incorporates what seems to be the first noteworthy result of this self-limitation to materialism. 'Materialist and Idealist' are *not* alternative terms for Coleridge's 'Aristotelian and Platonist.' In the Coleridgean distinction the gap represented is as great as that between traditional, critical, and creative (*cf.* p. 180, *ante*). But 'Materialist and Idealist'—as Mr. Richards himself suggests, are not so very far apart. They are two divisions in the realm of traditional philosophy, opposite ends of the same plane. Conversion from materialism to idealism is easily possible. Most athletic thinkers perform this feat more than once in their lives, one way or the other. But the change from 'Aristotle' to 'Plato' is an earthquake as terrible as that by which the bird breaks out of its egg. Seen as anything except an act of growth it loses its meaning. It is only 'materialism or idealism' which is a question of heads or tails. But the materialist cannot realise 'materialist to Platonist,' 'Aristotelian to Platonist,' as an act of *growth* without ceasing to be a materialist. In fact, if Coleridge's own words are to be taken literally, 'Materialist' cannot interpret 'Plato' at all.

I believe that Aristotle never could get to understand what Plato meant by an idea. . . . He was a conceptualist and never could raise himself into that higher state which was natural to Plato, and has been so to others, in which the understanding is distinctly contemplated, and, as it were, looked down upon from the throne of actual ideas, or living, inborn, essential truths.

And yet Mr. Richards interprets Coleridge with more than useful brilliance. It is only with the *process* of Coleridge's thought, with its evolution, that he disappoints. *Can* 'Coleridge on the Imagination' be fully understood without this element—without an account of Coleridge's deepening capacity for experience, and of the gradually more successful attempts to make those experiences conscious? There are smaller omissions, even errors. Mr. Richards epitomises the great Coleridgean change as 'Hartley into Kant.' But though Kant is right for 'idealist,' he is a bad symbol for the 'Platonist' metamorphosis which Coleridge experienced. Coleridge, indeed, exemplifies him as 'Aristotelian.' In Kant, he says, is to be found 'all of the philosophy that can be *learnt*.' To understand Kant no co-equality in crucial experience is necessary. 'Hartley into Spinoza' would be better. Kant was a way out, not a goal.

More awareness of the charts and processes of Coleridge's thought, also, would have prevented Mr. Richards showing him as a man who, like Wordsworth, experienced a few years of intense life and then decayed; whereas the truth is that after suffering a death-like interval (1804-11) Coleridge rose from the grave not to further growth but to further powers of expressiveness, deeper self-knowledge even, articulate over a wider range of thought than ever before.

Mr. Richards talks of 1816 as a time when Coleridge 'was writing as much from a memory of his thinking during this first creative period as from a renewed "act of contemplation." ' This judgment does not even apply to the last years of Coleridge's life. In the same way, failing to see Coleridge's life as a *life*, Mr. Richards cites Coleridge's Γνῶθι σεαυτόν poem of 1832:

> What is there in thee, Man, that can be known? . . .
> Ignore thyself and seek to know thy God!

And compares it with the 'Know Thyself' postulate of his 1816 philosophy, suggesting that the contrasting poem is the product of resignation and despair. Whereas in fact the alteration of the postulate into 'Know God' corresponds to an enlargement of Coleridge's conception of self, the outward sign of which is an alteration to a language of religion which he found in late life more expressive of his thought and used exclusively in defiance—unfortunate defiance— of the possibility that his words would be ignored as merely pious. In the verse lines he is actually reflecting a thought in one of his earliest poems:

> There is one mind, one omnipresent Mind
>   . . . with the which
> Who feeds and saturates his constant soul,
> He from his small particular orbit flies,
> With blest outstarting! From himself he flies. . . .

He is speaking, in the two passages, of different kinds of 'self.'[1]

---

[1] Another kind of God, Mr. Richards suggests. His assertion of disillusion in Coleridge is undogmatic.

I believe that if Mr. Richards were really a pollarded 'Aristotle' materialist there would be more serious misjudgments of this kind. As it is, I think the 'materialism' is confined to Mr. Richards' manners, as it were, or to his tone of voice. A sensible-scientific air is imparted; there is a certain detached clarity which, applied to Coleridge's kind of clarity, seems strange, or confusing. Mr. Richards, for instance, scientifically takes nothing for granted. Excellent—but in some contexts distracting. It is strange in this particular context—in the pages, for instance, on Coleridge's 'Know Thyself' implication—to find a paragraph devoted to the reminder that introspection is not involved. Or when the subject of Nature is to be discussed, in the context of Coleridge's poetic apprehension of it, we need not have been prepared for the clarifying analysis which follows by the reminder that 'Nature . . . has too often been taken as the mere reflection of a taste for certain types of scenery. . . . It goes, of course, infinitely beyond this.'

Then the march of the reader will be interrupted, or rather the reader, used to Coleridge territory, will feel as if he was suddenly walking with right foot in left-hand slipper, left in right, when he finds the materialist conception of philosophy turning up—the conception of philosophy as a great and ever-enlarging palace, existing by itself, with philosophers the architects, the plumbers, the improvers. 'There can be little doubt,' says Mr. Richards suddenly, 'that Coleridge as against Associationism of the Hartley-Condillac type was right all along the line.' It is as if Coleridge had superseded an effete system of ringing for chambermaids. What would Coleridge have said to that 'was right'? The extraordinary thing about the Palace of Philosophy is that one day it will be completed. The time will undoubtedly come, Mr. Richards infers, after a few more Coleridges (p. 127), when we shall be able by analysis and argument to *settle* the merits and demerits of a piece of poetry. The Criticism Wing is nearing completion.

It is not, I think, that Mr. Richards writes as a materialist so much as that he seems to be writing for nameless materialist friends, for the sake of whom he appears almost to want to disassociate himself from some of the inescapably non-materialist aspects of his subjects. He is careful to point out when he writes of 'feelings' that he means nothing nebulous, or vaguely warm. Is rigidly detached when he talks, as he often has to, about the 'inner sense.' It is as if he were anxious not to estrange some invisible audience of Aristotelians. He has to admit that Coleridge was a 'resolute freewill man' (though I should suggest that the determination native to the meaning of the epithet 'resolute' is foreign to Coleridge's kind of 'freewill'). But in making this admission, he is glad to be able to make him 'more acceptable to determinist eyes,' to find 'a possible plank by means of which a determinist can go across into Coleridge's freewill territory.' Whereupon he defines freewill with profound understanding of the meaning Coleridge gave to it, in thought not far from Coleridge's definition of faith (quoted here on p. 228) which Mr. Richards does not know. But these planks, these means of approach, allow only spatial contiguity. An oak can approach extremely near the owls on its branches without beginning to understand them: these planks can only be walked, because they only exist, in the scaffolding of the materialist's palace of philosophy. For the true materialist to understand what Coleridge means by freewill no amount of broad-mindedness will avail. He must retrace his way to the point of divergence, most near to the root of 'Plato' and 'Aristotle.' Still more tact is necessary to present for the materialist what it is that Coleridge means, exactly, precisely, when he uses the verb, so tremendous and reverberant in the mouth of the 'Platonist,' so trite in philosophical palaces—the verb 'to know.' Mr. Richards reserves a chapter for it—he chooses to describe it, following Coleridge, as that act in which subject and object become merged. Enlarging on it, he utters a warning:

> The coalescence of the Subject and the Object in the act of knowing is a difficult doctrine—partly because it needs practising, partly because other senses of *Subject* and *Object* (and still more of *subjective* and *objective*) are so easily confused with these.

Will not this mislead some of his readers? 'Many senses of subject and object'—true, and Mr. Richards goes on to enumerate some of them. But is not this just the kind of explanation that the materialist may not safely be trusted with? Will he not believe that if he can only be sure, as he feels now he can be sure, that he is coalescing object, in its relevant signification, with subject, in *its* relevant signification, then there is nothing to prevent him 'knowing' as Coleridge knew? All that is necessary, as Mr. Richards says, is practice. Again—dangerous phrase. Not necessarily the wrong phrase, but not best chosen for breaking to materialist readers the fact that an order of activity is here under consideration for which in their own philosophy there is no place. It may be possible to 'practise' growth, it may even be possible to practise that not dis-related process of transformation by which Saul becomes Paul, but it is a misleading word for the audience for whom Mr. Richards seems to be writing.

In short, the comment which a first reading of this book calls out is that here are the dangers (though not the disasters) of external clarification. I have an uneasy feeling that it is the first comment which all first readings of Mr. Richards calls forth, and that it has been answered often enough already. But then, perhaps, the very eloquence of Mr. Richards in emphasising the importance of giving precision to critical terms has made it already necessary to point out the dangers of this precision, especially as applied to Coleridge— To point out that this precise meaning is a metaphysical abstraction only unless it is exact because it is an exact reflection of drift, and that it cannot be understood except by those who have a precise apprehension of this drift. In describing Coleridge's 'poetical,' or 'æsthetic' experience, his 'experience from nature,' Mr. Richards would help us to understand this experience, and Coleridge's account of it, by giving precision to the meaning of the most usefully indeterminate of all words—'Nature.' But does his '1, 2, 3, 4' analysis of nature, which we lean back and read in lazy gratitude that we have had it all thought out for us, really help readers to know better what Coleridge means in the Æolian Harp passage? It gives an intellectual description (one can state this without the faintest desire to denigrate intellectualism in the modern manner) of an event which is not susceptible to such interpretation. Such a passage is understood up to the experience of each individual reader. For those co-experiencers to whom the event has meaning, the explanation will be unnecessary, and only valuable as something of pleasing polish and balance: for those to whom the experience has no meaning, the explanation will seem to confer an understanding which in fact it does not.

So it comes about that any reader of Mr. Richards, better educated in his thought than in his life, may find himself deceived into the belief that he has 'got' what Coleridge means, whereas all that he has 'got' is a Coleridge in terms of his own intellectual education —a Coleridge still considerably important but shorn of the Coleridge differentials, of the New which Coleridge contributed to the world. Mr. Richards ought to take care that his readers are feeling as clearly as they are being made to think—for it is the true Coleridge which Mr. Richards is able to describe. But sometimes he himself forgets Coleridge's test for a valid philosophy—does it tell you something in the heart? Sometimes he stares so long at the terms before him, under so strong a light, that the amount of meaning in each word seems the same—the meaning seems the same. 'It can easily be assumed,' he says by way of retrospective summary at the end of a chapter, 'that Coleridge's doctrine of the mind as a self-realising activity and Locke's (or James Mill's) view of it as a combination of impressions, ideas and movements, are necessarily in conflict with one another.' But can we be sure, he goes on, until we have a technique of comparison more perfect than anything we have so far been able to come within distant hail of, that the difference is not merely in the vocabularies? And until this is so, ought we not to be 'chary of deciding that there is any irreconcilable clash between their results'? Intellectual integrity must extort a terrible price if it leads to doubt as to the validity of distinctions so absolute. Mr. Richards is momentarily using philosophy in the way Coleridge said that it should never be used—'to perplex our clearest notions and living moral instincts.' In the palace of philosophy everything must be of the same order, inorganic brick-matter. You cannot build with material which is still living. The organic material of the Coleridgean philosophy must be made amenable for building purposes. Coleridge himself must be presented as a fellow architect. In this study of Coleridge's philosophy we are encouraged to make an effort of thought comparable to that made by its founder, to remember that Coleridge was a trained student (p. 37) and that what he has to say will not be understood except by those with similar training, to remember that 'the chief weakness of our best criticism to-day is the pretence that fundamental matters can be profitably discussed without prolonged and technical thinking.' And yet Mr. Richards knows that this is not true—*or rather* that it is not the point that needs emphasis, is the last point which needs emphasis in the study of Coleridge. Not prolonged and technical thinking but intense and arduous living, or some intuition of it, is necessary for the 'profitable discussion of fundamental matters,' is necessary for the understanding of Coleridge, is the power of Coleridge, in whom thought and arduous living were one.

It is these very powers of Coleridge, the fact that

with him thought is growth, feeling is growth, that Mr. Richards makes clear. I should like to try to do justice to this fact, which makes *Coleridge on the Imagination* perhaps the best book on Coleridge which has yet appeared, with scarcely a loose phrase, or an unpondered judgment in it, and the emphasis laid *for the first time* exclusively on that part of Coleridge's work which is most likely to be thought important by, which is itself formative of, the future. The sensible-materialist tone (which perhaps doesn't appear enough to matter) seems half put on, as if its author were conscious of some unseen materialist monitor, approving or disapproving from his corner. Or perhaps, to take an analogy from 'Coleridge and S.T.C.,' it is only Mr. Richards' 'I.A.R.' which admonishes him to preserve, besides his magnificent discipline of thought, a defensive discipline only necessary for those who, unlike Mr. Richards, have nothing important to say.

LIST OF REFERENCES

Numbers not preceded by a letter refer to the
Nonesuch *Coleridge*, ed. Stephen Potter, 1933.

A.D.S.   *Coleridge's Cosmogony*, by A. D. Snyder, 1924.
A.D.Sn.   *The Critical Principle of the Reconciliation of Opposites
            as employed by Coleridge*, by A. D. Snyder, 1918.
A.G.L.   *The Literary Life . . . of W. Harness*, by A. G.
            L'Estrange, 1871.
A.P.   *Anima Poetae*, ed. E. H. Coleridge, 1895.
A.R.   *Aids to Reflection*.
B.E.   *Biographia Epistolaris*, ed. A. Turnbull, 1911.
B.L.   *Biographia Literaria*, ed. J. Shawcross, 1907.
C.   *Confessions of an Enquiring Spirit*.
C.   *Early Recollections*, by J. Cottle.
C.S.   *On the Constitution of Church and State*, ed. H. N.
            Coleridge, 1839.
D.S.   *Dorothy Wordsworth*, by E. De Sélincourt, 1933.
E.V.L.   *Charles Lamb and the Lloyds*, by E. V. Lucas.
H.C.R.   *Correspondence . . . with the Wordsworth Circle*, H. Crabb
            Robinson, 1927.
H.C.Rob.   *Blake, Coleridge . . . etc.*, H. Crabb Robinson, 1922.
J.D.   *Memoirs of the Life of Sir Humphry Davy*, by J. Davy,
            1836.
J.D.C.   *Life of Samuel Taylor Coleridge*, by J. D. Campbell,
            1893.
J.H.M.   *Coleridge as Philosopher*, by J. H. Muirhead, 1930.
J.L.L.   *The Road to Xanadu*, by J. L. Lowes, 1931.
K.   *Letters of the Wordsworth Family*, ed. Knight.
L.   *Letters of Samuel Taylor Coleridge*, ed. E. H. Cole-
            ridge, 1895.
L.R.   *Literary Remains*, ed. H. N. Coleridge, 1836.
L.S.   *History of English Thought in the Eighteenth Century*,
            by Leslie Stephen.

LIST OF REFERENCES

M.	Marginal notes quoted *London Mercury*, September 1926.
MS.	All MS. extracts are taken from the collections of the British Museum, except
MS. G.H.B.	From the collection of the Rev. G. H. B. Coleridge.
P.	*Poetical Works*, ed. E. H. Coleridge, 1912.
R.B.L.	*Tom Wedgwood*, by R. B. Litchfield, 1903.
R,S.	*Life and Correspondence of Robert Southey*, ed. C. C. Southey, 1849–
S.	*Thomas Poole and His Friends*, by Mrs. Sandford.
S.C.	*Shakespearean Criticism*, ed. T. M. Raysor, 1930.
S.M.	*The Statesman's Manual.*
S.P.	*Minnow among Tritons* (letters of Mrs. Coleridge), ed. S. Potter, 1934.
T.M.R.	*Coleridge and Asra*, by T. M. Raysor, *Studies in Philology*, July 1929.
U.L.	*Unpublished Letters of Samuel Taylor Coleridge*, ed. E. L. Griggs, 1932.
W.H.	*Early Life of Robert Southey*, by W. Haller, 1917.

INDEX

INDEX

Goethe, 18, 22, 91, 185, 194, 215, 218, 250, 261
Green, J. H., 72, 80, 174

Hamlet, 111, 140-2, 179
Hartley, 33, 35, 43, 47, 106, 134, 199, 221, 230, 269
Hazlitt, 15, 31, 46, 86, 119, 120, 154, 157, 166, 176, 256
Hints Towards the Formation of a More Comprehensive Theory of Life, 193
Hume, 43, 181, 186, 199, 203, 208-9, 217, 247-8, 250, 256
Hutchinson, Sarah, 58

Iago, 138
Irving, Edward, 77, 174

Jeffrey, 120, 154, 159
Johnson, Dr., 37, 128, 138, 183, 193, 246
Junius, 126

Kant, 24, 41-3, 179, 181, 185, 269, 271
Keats, 97, 99, 151, 202
Kubla Khan, 63

Lamb, 38, 42, 77, 89, 90, 99, 128, 149, 157, 163-6, 171
Leibnitz, 33, 181
Leighton, Archbishop, 126, 134
Letters on the Inspiration of the Scriptures, 224
Lewin, Dr., 67
Lewis, 'Monk,' 91
Locke, 29, 33, 199, 277
Love, 87, 149
Lover's Resolutions, The, 233
Luther, 136, 219
Lyrical Ballads, Preface, 170

Mackintosh, Sir James, 154, 182
Malthus, 184

Milton, 137, 148
Moore, Tom, 91, 155
Morgans, the, 72, 173
Muirhead, J. H., 23, 177, 188, 222

Nelson, 137, 239
Newton, 35
Nurse, the (in *Romeo and Juliet*), 122

Ode to Dejection, 51, 146, 150
Omniana, 184
Osorio, 40, 98

Paley, 184, 221, 248
Pecksniff, 95, 115
Plato, 45
Poems, 145-52
Poole, 38, 71, 100-1, 124, 162, 167-8, 211, 246
Pope, 193
Priestley, 28, 36, 221, 256

Radcliffe, Mrs., 246, 249
Rasselas, Prince, 249
Religious Musings, 35, 76, 146, 163
Remorse, 72
Richard II., 82
Richards, I. A., 134, 175, 265-79
Robinson, H. Crabb, 87, 98, 140, 169, 171, 221
Rogers, Sam, 154-5

Schelling, 42, 75, 179, 185
Schiller, 32, 41, 83
Scott, 107-8
Shakespeare, 91, 134, 137-42, 144, 238
Shawcross, 23, 177
Sherlock, 238, 247
Shotover, Captain, 63
Smalbroke, Bishop, 247
Snyder, A. D., 177
Southey, R., 30, 38, 62, 92, 94, 98, 110, 120, 156-7, 162, 256
Spinoza, 41-3, 165, 185, 234, 271

284

INDEX